Hip-Hop Poetry and The Classics

by

Alan Sitomer & Michael Cirelli

Connecting our classic curriculum to Hip-Hop poetry through standards-based, language arts instruction.

The Classics	The Contemporaries
Tennyson	Tupac
Keats	Run DMC
Frost	Public Enemy
Dickinson	Mos Def
Hughes	Nas
Shakespeare	Eminem
Kipling	Taleb Kweli
Poe	KRS-1
Shelley	Notorious B.I.G.
Plath	Common
Blake	Ice Cube

With Academic Material for...

AP Exams
Gifted and Talented Education
English Language Learners
Recitals and Slams
Vocabulary Enrichment
&
All English Classes Teaching Poetry

Hip-Hop Poetry and The Classics

Our goal is to make the academic study of poetry accessible, relevant, comprehensible and enjoyable to students in our contemporary, multicultural classrooms.

Our methodology* is to analyze the poetry of Hip-Hop and compare its motifs, themes, and general poetic devices (such as alliteration, rhyme scheme, figurative language, etc. …) to the "classic" poems traditionally studied (by writers such as Frost, Dickinson, Keats, etc. …) in order to teach the core elements of the poetic craft in an appealing, relevant, thorough and accessible manner.

Our aim is to dispel preconceived notions about poetry for students and educators alike.

- *For Students:* Our aim is to convert the traditional response to the idea of studying poetry from, "Poetry?… *YUCK!*" to an appreciation of the writing as well as the art form.

- *For Educators:* Our aim is to convert the traditional response to the idea of studying Hip-Hop from, "Hip-Hop? You mean those thugs and *gangstas*?" to an appreciation of the writing as well as the art form.

And we pledge to be free of *edubabble*.

* This text has been aligned to 38 different California Language Arts Standards.

Copyright ©2004 by Alan Lawrence Sitomer
All Rights Reserved

ISBN #: 0-9721882-2-3

First Edition, First Printing
Printed in Canada
by Milk Mug Publishing
9190 West Olympic Blvd.
Suite 253
Beverly Hills, CA 90212
(310) 278-1153

Page Design, Typography, and PrePress by Kathleen Weisel (weiselcreative.com)
Cover Design: Taaron Silverstein

Visit us on the web: www.HipHopintheClass.com

Acknowledgments

For permission to reprint copyrighted material, grateful acknowledgment is made to the sources cited on page 157. Their generosity and kindness of spirit is both notable and admirable. Improving literacy on a national level is ALL of our concerns and the contributions made by the Hip-Hop community, music publishers, poets, book publishing companies and artists themselves in the name of education are to be saluted. We thank you.

CONTENTS
Core Literary Elements

Alliteration 6
   Interpretation Guide 6
   WRITING EXERCISE 7

Allusion 8
   Ain't I a Woman? by Sojourner Truth 8
      Interpretation Guide 9
      Student Worksheet 11
   For Women by Talib Kweli 12
      Interpretation Guide 13
      Student Worksheet 14
   WRITING EXERCISE 15

Epitaph 16
   WRITING EXERCISE 17

Figurative Language 18

Haiku 19

Hyperbole 20
      Interpretation Guide 20
   WRITING EXERCISE 21

Imagery 22
   Harlem: A Dream Deferred by Langston Hughes 22
      Interpretation Guide 23
      Student Worksheet 24
   Juicy by Notorious B.I.G 25
      Interpretation Guide 26
      Student Worksheet 27
   WRITING EXERCISE 28

Irony 29
   The Fish by Elizabeth Bishop 29
      Interpretation Guide 30
      Student Worksheet 31

Meaning 32
   Do Not Go Gentle Into That Good Night by Dylan Thomas 32
      Interpretation Guide 33
      Student Worksheet 34
   Me Against the World by Tupac Shakur 35
      Interpretation Guide 36
      Student Worksheet 37
      Compare & Contrast 38
   WRITING EXERCISE 39

Metaphors 40
   The Weaver by Anonymous 40
      Interpretation Guide 41
      Student Worksheet 42
   Respiration by Mos Def 43
      Interpretation Guide 44
      Student Worksheet 45
   WRITING EXERCISE 46

Mood 47
   We Real Cool by Gwendolyn Brooks 47
      Interpretation Guide 48
      Student Worksheet 49

A Roller Skating Jam by De La Soul / *Follow Me* by Sage Francis . . . 50
    Interpretation Guide 51
    Student Worksheet 52
  WRITING EXERCISE 53

Onomatopoeia 54
  The Congo by Vachel Lindsay 54
    Interpretation Guide 55
    Student Worksheet 56
  Datskat by The Roots 57
    Interpretation Guide 58
    Student Worksheet 59
  WRITING EXERCISE 60

Pattern 61
  If by Rudyard Kipling 61
    Interpretation Guide 62
    Student Worksheet 64
  How Many by Zion I 65
    Interpretation Guide 66
    Student Worksheet 67
  WRITING EXERCISE 68

Personification 69
  Lodged by Robert Frost 69
    Interpretation Guide 70
    Student Worksheet 71
  Mirror by Sylvia Plath / *I Am Music* by Common 72
    Interpretation Guide 73
    Compare & Contrast 74
    Student Worksheet 75
  WRITING EXERCISE 76

Rhyme Schemes 77

Simile 79
  WRITING EXERCISE 80

Sonnets 81
  Another Sonnet for Stephan by Alvin Lester Sitomer 81
    Interpretation Guide 82
    Student Worksheet 85
    Answer Key 86
  WRITING EXERCISE 87

Symbolism 88
  Sympathy by Paul Laurence Dunbar 88
    Interpretation Guide 89
    Student Worksheet 90
  Three Strikes You In by Ice Cube 92
    Interpretation Guide 93
    Student Worksheet 94
  WRITING EXERCISE 95

Tone 96
  The Night Has a Thousand Eyes by Francis Bourdillon 96
    Interpretation Guide 97
    Student Worksheet 98
  Paid In Full by Rakim 99
    Interpretation Guide 100
    Student Worksheet 101
  WRITING EXERCISE 102

Additional Poetic Resources

Reading Strategies 104
   Jabberwocky by Lewis Carroll 104
      Interpretation Guide 105
      Student Worksheet 107

Author's Choice – Classic
   The Tide Rises, The Tide Falls by Henry Wadsworth Longfellow 108
      Interpretation Guide 109
      Student Worksheet 110

Author's Choice – Hip-Hop 111
   Fight the Power by Public Enemy 111
      Interpretation Guide 112
      Student Worksheet 113
   Otha Fish by The Pharcyde 114
      Interpretation Guide 115
      Student Worksheet 116
   Lose Yourself by Eminem 117
      Interpretation Guide 118
      Student Worksheet 119

Recital Exercises 120
   Memorizing and Performing 120
      Love's Philosophy by Percy Bysshe Shelley 121
   Oral Interpretations 122
   Assuming an Identity 123
   Performing Team Poems 124
   How to Host a Poetry Slam 125

Activities 126
   Acrostics 126
   Autobiographical Poem 127
   Simile and Metaphors 129
   Create a Poetry Journal 130
   Poetry Journal Grading Rubric 131
   Hip-Hop Poetry Word Search / Word Scramble / Answer Key 132

AP Exam Success 135
   Initial Strategy 135
   Multiple Choice Strategy 136
   Essay Questions Strategy 137
   Sample Essay Prompt: William Shakespeare's *Sonnet 18* 138
   Sample Essay Answer Rubric 139

Gifted and Talented Education 141
   Differentiated Lessons 141

English Language Learners 143
   Bridging Comprehension 143

Extended Writing Activities 144
   Create A Diamante Poem 144
   Food As A Metaphor For Ourselves 145
   Rewriting For Meaning 146
   Rewriting For Opposite Imagery 147
   The Alliterative Day In A Life 148

Appendix

Glossary of Terms 150
California Language Arts Standards 151

Enlightening Alliteration
Interpretation Guide

CA Language Arts Standards Covered:
9/10 LRA 3.7; L&S 1.1; 11/12 R 2.0, 2.2; LRA 3.4

Alliteration: The repetition of the same or similar consonant sounds in words that are close together.

For example:

> Behemoth, biggest born of earth, upheaved his vastness.
> (John Milton)

Almost every great poet has used the technique of alliteration to add beauty and musicality to their works.

For example:

> We passed the Fields of *Gazing Grain*—
> We passed the *Setting Sun*—
> (Emily Dickinson)

> *Brazen bells*!
> What a *tale* of *terror*, now, *their turbulency tells*!
> (Edgar Allen Poe)

> In Xanadu did *Kubla Khan*
> A stately pleasure *dome decree*:
> Where Alph, the sacred *river*, *ran*
> Through caverns *measureless* to *man*
> Down to a *sunless sea*.
> (Samuel Taylor Coleridge)

Almost every great Hip-Hop poet has used the technique of alliteration to add beauty and musicality to their works.

For example:

> I'm the *Ladies Love*, *legend* in *leather*
> *Long* and *lean*, and I don't wear *pleather*
> (LL Cool J)

> *Peter Piper picked peppers*
> but *Run rocked rhymes*
> (Run DMC)

> *Representin'* the West, *relevant* to *relentless* sentences.
> If *renegade rebels resent* this wicked syntax
> *Revert* to *revolution Ras reverses*, *reverberates*
> *revolvin'* with written *retaliation*...
> (Ras Kass)

Poetry Writing Exercise: Alliteration

Learning Objective: Students will identify and utilize the poetic device of alliteration.
Standards Addressed: 9/10 W&O 1.3, 1.4; LRA 3.7, 11/12 W&O 1.1, 1.2
Materials needed: This worksheet.
Methodology: See below.

Identify the alliteration in the following sentences. Underline alike letters.

For example:

Snakes **s**lither **s**lowly on the **s**idewalk.

1. Jumping Jennifer jammed Johnny's jaw full of jellybeans.
2. Silly Susan swims under the summer sun.
3. Pretty Paula pounced on Penelope's purple pancake.

Finish these sentences using alliteration.

1. Terrific Tony _____ .
2. English earmuffs _____ .
3. Black bears and brown bugs _____ .

Tongue Twisters are built on Alliteration.
Try to recite some of the following aloud.

- Peter Piper picked a peck of pickled peppers.
- Black bug's blood.
- Mrs. Smith's Fish Sauce Shop.
- Shy Shelly says she shall sew sheets.
- Three free throws.
- Knapsack straps.
- Which wristwatches are Swiss wristwatches?
- Greek grapes.
- One smart fellow, he felt smart.
  Two smart fellows, they felt smart.
  Three smart fellows, they all felt smart.

Create three of your own tongue twisters using alliteration.

1. _____ .
2. _____ .
3. _____ .

Alliteration can get kind of crazy. See how long of a sentence you can create using alliteration. The meaning of the sentences should make sense (at least, a little).

For example:

The *powers* of *prunes* are *prudent* to *provide potent pallitive prophylaxis* of *potential pooper problems, priming* you for *purging*.
(*Rob Bohnenberger*)

_____
_____
_____ .

Uncovering Allusion – Classic

Ain't I a Woman?

by Sojourner Truth

1   That man over there say
    A woman needs to be helped into carriages
    And lifted over ditches
    And to have the best place everywhere.
5   Nobody ever helped me into carriages
    Or over mud puddles
    Or gives me a best place.
    And ain't I a woman?

    Look at me, Look at my arm!
10   I have plowed and planted
    and gathered into barns
    And no man could head me
    And ain't I a woman?

    I could work as much
15   and eat as much as a man—
    When I could get to it—
    and bear the lash as well
    and ain't I a woman?

    I have born 13 children
20   and seen most all sold into slavery
    and when I cried out a mother's grief
    none but Jesus heard me
    and ain't I a woman?

    That little man in black there say
25   woman can't have as much rights as a man
    cause Christ wasn't a woman
    Where did your Christ come from?
    From God and a woman!
    Man had nothing to do with him!
30   If the first woman God ever made
    was strong enough to turn the world
    upside down, all alone
    together women ought to be able to turn it
    rightside up again.

Uncovering Allusion – Classic
Interpretation Guide

CA Language Arts Standards Covered:
   9/10 R 2.0; LRA 3.4, 3.7, 3.12; L&S 1.1; 9/10 W&O 1.3, 1.4; 11/12 LRA 3.2, 3.4, 3.8; R 2.5; W 2.2; W&O 1.1, 1.2

Allusion: A reference to someone or something that is known from history, literature, religion, politics, sports, science, or some other branch of culture.

Poetic Theme: Equality of Race & Sex

Sojourner Truth's poem is filled with allusions.
Have students identify what the author is referring to in the following lines:

Line 1: Who is the "man" to which the author refers?

The "man" could be a literal, specific person such as a political figure in the author's time that was overtly withholding women's rights. (This would most likely be a white man as white men were the power brokers of the era and this poem later addresses the theme of slavery in addition to gender equality).

The "man" could also be an example of figurative language whereby the idea of "the man" as oppressor was a symbol of all those (white) men who withheld political rights and power from people of race and a different gender.

Line 6: What is the author alluding to, "Or over mud puddles"?

This could be an allusion to the well known story of the unnamed gentleman who gallantly laid his coat over a mud puddle for a fine lady to step on so that she did not get her feet dirty while exiting a carriage. The allusion shows how the author herself has never been the benefactor of men's gallantry. It is inferred that this is due to her race. (The author is black and the woman in the famed story is supposedly white.)

Line 10: What does the author mean, "I have plowed and planted"?

This is an allusion to her time spent working in the fields as a black slave owned by a white plantation owner. This line exemplifies a history of oppression against her race.

Line 12: Explain the line, "And no man could head me."

This is an allusion to the fact that the author could equal the work of any man out there working in the field with her and that her gender as a woman never meant she was capable of doing less work. This line exemplifies a history of oppression against her gender.

Line 24: Who is the "little man in black" to which the author refers?

Most probably this is an allusion to a preacher, a priest, or a man of religious power. The history of oppression has a long list of people who claimed they were using "God's word" as a reason to justify their oppression of other people.

Ironically, the "little man in black" is most probably a white man.

Line 28 & 29: To what famous moment is the author alluding?

The author is referring to the Virgin Birth of Jesus.

Line 30, 31 & 32: To what other famous moment is the author alluding?

The author is referring to Eve leading Adam to take a bite of the Forbidden Fruit (i.e., the apple) in the Garden of Eden.

Uncovering Allusion – Classic
Interpretation Guide *continued*

Line 33 & 34: What "call to action" is the author putting forth for all women to embrace if the world is to be turned "rightside up again"?

The author is making reference to the idea that women need to unify behind the cause of terminating the oppression that is keeping them unequal to men in society if they are ever going to have equal standing.

What is your impression of the author of this poem after exploring some of the allusions in her poem "Ain't I a Woman?"

- She is intelligent.
- She knows her history.
- She is passionate.
- She is trying to encourage other woman to stand up for their rights.

Uncovering Allusion – Classic
Student Worksheet

Allusion: A reference to someone or something that is known from history, literature, religion, politics, sports, science, or some other branch of culture.

Sojourner Truth's poem is filled with allusions. Identify what the author refers to in lines:

Line 1: Who is the "man" to which the author refers?

_____

_____

Line 6: What is the author alluding to, "Or over mud puddles"?

_____

_____

Line 10: What does the author mean, "I have plowed and planted"?

_____

_____

Line 12: Explain the line, "And no man could head me."

_____

_____

Line 24: Who is the "little man in black" to which the author refers?

_____

Line 28 & 29: To what famous moment is the author alluding?

_____

_____

Line 30, 31 & 32: To what other famous moment is the author alluding?

_____

_____

Line 33 & 34: What "call to action" is the author putting forth for all women to embrace if the world is to be turned "right side up again"?

_____

_____

What is your impression of the author of this poem after exploring some of the allusions in her poem "Ain't I a Woman?"

_____

_____

Uncovering Allusion – Hip-Hop

For Women

by Talib Kweli

1   A daughter come up in Georgia, ripe and ready to plant seeds,
Left the plantation when she saw a sign even though she can't read
It came from God and when life get hard she always speak to him,
She'd rather kill her babies than let the master get to 'em,

5   She on the run up north to get across the Mason-Dixon
In church she learned how to be patient and keep wishin',
The promise of eternal life after death for those that God bless
She swears the next baby she'll have, will breathe a free breath
And get milk from a free breast,
10   And love being alive,
Otherwise they'll have to give up being themselves to survive…

Some will grow to be old women, some will die before they born,
They'll be mothers and lovers who inspire and make songs,
But me, my skin is brown and my manner is tough,
15   Like the love I give my babies when the rainbow's enuff,
I aint got time to lie, my life has been much too rough,
Still running with bare feet, I aint got nothin' but my soul,
Freedom is the ultimate goal,
Life and death is small on the whole, in many ways
20   I'm awfully bitter these days
Because the only parents God gave me, they were slaves,
And it crippled me, I got the destiny of a casualty,
And I live through my babies and I change my reality

Maybe one day I'll ride back to Georgia on a train,
25   Folks 'round there call me Peaches, I guess that's my name.

Uncovering Allusion – Hip-Hop
Interpretation Guide

CA Language Arts Standards Covered:
    9/10 R 3.0; LRA 3.2, 3.4, 3.7, 3.10, 3.12; L&S 1.1; W&O 1.4; W 2.2; 11/12 LRA 3.2, 3.4, 3.8; R 2.5; W&O 1.1, 1.2; W 2.2

Allusion: A reference to someone or something that is known from
history, literature, religion, politics, sports, science, or some other branch of culture.

Poetic Theme: Equality of Race & Sex

Talib Kweli's lyrics are filled with allusions.
Have students identify what the author is referring to in the following lines:

Line 1 & 2: What is the poet alluding to in these lines?

The poet is referencing the slave plantations and the industry of slavery in the South, specifically Georgia in this instance. "Ripe and ready to plant seeds," is a direct allusion to the type of work that was bestowed upon the slaves in the plantation. It is also interesting to point out that the subject "saw a sign even though she can't read," because slaves were kept from education in these times. This is an example of the savage inequalities that occurred in our nation's history.

Line 5: Explain the reference to the Mason-Dixon?

This is an historical allusion to the Mason-Dixon Line, the border between the slave states and the free states before the Civil War ended slavery. The Mason-Dixon Line was the destination many slaves hoped to reach as they tried to escape to freedom.

Line 15: What is the poet referring to in the line, "when the rainbow's enuff"?

This is a reference to popular literature, "For Colored Girls Who Have Considered Suicide *When The Rainbow's Enuff,*" by Ntozake Shange. This piece of literature is actually an extended prose poem that has been performed all over the country dealing with the difficulties of being African-American and female in our society.

COMPARE & CONTRAST: *Classic Poetry to Hip-Hop*

Sojourner Truth is a celebrated, famous poet who has received great recognition for her literary efforts. Talib Kweli is a skillful, Hip-Hop poet whose work is largely unknown outside the contemporary world of Hip-Hop music. Do you feel that the work of Kweli deserves the same type of "literary merit and attention" that the work of Truth does? Why?

> *ANSWERS WILL VARY but some possible points mentioned will be...*

- They are both intelligent, they know their history, they are passionate and they are trying to enlighten and inspire women of color.

Do you feel that the work of contemporary Hip-Hop poets in general get the positive recognition they deserve? Why or why not?

> *ANSWERS WILL VARY but some possible points mentioned will be...*

- No, Hip-Hop poets are NOT recognized for their skill and literary merit. Hip-Hop poets are considered "shallow" due to misperceptions by larger society. These misperceptions include that Hip-Hop is solely filled with "Gangstas," that Hip-Hop poets are not intelligent and that Hip-Hop poets are not aware/do not understand the works of "classic poets." All of these are untrue.

Uncovering Allusion – Hip-Hop
Student Worksheet

Allusion: A reference to someone or something that is known from
history, literature, religion, politics, sports, science, or some other branch of culture.

Talib Kweli's lyrics are filled with allusions.
Identify what the author is referring to in the following lines:

Line 1 & 2: What is the poet alluding to in these lines?

_____

_____

_____

Line 5: Explain the reference to the Mason-Dixon?

_____

_____

_____

Line 15: What is the poet referring to in the line, "when the rainbow's enuff"?

_____

_____

_____

COMPARE AND CONTRAST: Classic Poetry to Hip-Hop

Materials needed:

  Ain't I a Woman? by S. Truth
  &
  For Women by Talib Kweli

1. **Sojourner Truth is a celebrated, famous poet who has received great recognition for her literary efforts. Talib Kweli is a skillful, Hip-Hop poet whose work is largely unknown outside the contemporary world of Hip-Hop music. Do you feel that the work of Kweli deserves the same type of "literary merit and attention" that the work of Truth does? Why?**

2. **Do you feel that the work of contemporary Hip-Hop poets in general get the positive recognition they deserve? Why or why not?**

Poetry Writing Exercise: Allusion

Learning Objective: Students will identify and utilize the poetic device of allusion.
Standards addressed: 9/10 W&O 1.3, 1.4; LRA 3.7, 11/12 W&O 1.1, 1.2; W 2.2
Materials needed: This worksheet.
Methodology: See below.

Create a list of personal allusions using your own personal slang. Choose from the following list:

- **Loot**
- **School**
- **Food**
- **Your neighborhood**
- **Yourself**
- **Your friends**

- **The local market**
- **Telephone**
- **Computers**
- **Parents**
- **Brothers/sisters**
- **Teachers**

- **Basketball**
- **Kissing**
- **Sleep**
- **Work**
- **Cars**
- **Music**

I use _____ as a slang name for _____ .
    (*example:* **loot** = money)

I use _____ as a slang name for _____ .
    (*example:* **Echo Park** = my neighborhood)

I use _____ as a slang name for _____ .
    (*example:* **gran** = grandmother)

I use _____ as a slang name for _____ .
    (*example:* **ride** = car)

Now take the four slang names from the list (i.e., you have just crafted a list of personal allusions) and use them to construct a four-line, rhyming poem, using your own voice.

For example:

> I came into the kitchen and said, "What's shakin' gran?"
> She said, "I'm leaving Echo Park with a master plan.
> I've been saving all my loot every week.
> I'm going to buy a brand new ride,
> I'm in the driver's seat!"

My Personal Allusion Poem

_____

_____

_____

_____

_____

_____

Epitaphs

CA Language Arts Standards Covered:
9/10 LRA 3.7; L&S 1.1; 11/12 LRA 3.1; R 2.0

Epitaph: A brief poem written to be inscribed on a gravestone.

**Epitaphs come in many forms.
There are:**

Religious epitaphs...

> Wither, 0 wither should I fly
> But to my loving Saviours breast
> Secure within thy arms to lie
> And safe beneath thy wings to rest

Clever epitaphs...

> To follow you I'm not content.
> How do I know which way you went?
> *(Poet H.J. Daniel's epitaph for his wife)*

> I made an ash of myself.
> *(Ruth Adams)*

> Here lies an honest lawyer,
> and that is Strange.
> *(A lawyer named John Strange)*

Humorous epitaphs...

> Here lies my wife: here let her lie!
> Now she's at rest, and so am I.

> "I told you I was sick!"
> *(found in a Georgia cemetery)*

Famous Epitaphs...

> On the whole, I'd rather be in Philadelphia.
> *(W.C. Fields)*

One of the most famous epitaphs is that of William Shakespeare.

> Good Friends, for Jesus' sake forbear,
> To dig the bones enclosed here!
> Blest be the man that spares these stones,
> And curst be he that moves my bones.

A LITTLE HISTORY

When graveyards were full during Shakespeare's era, old corpses were often dug up to create space for the burial of new bodies. In addition, grave robbers sometimes dug up corpses to plunder them—especially if the person was wealthy or famous. Not a fan of these activities, Shakespeare wrote his own epitaph to scare would be "diggers" off. People's fear of superstition worked as his grave has survived unmolested for hundreds of years.

Poetry Writing Exercise: Epitaph

Learning Objective: Students will identify and utilize the poetic device of creating an epitaph.
Standards addressed: 9/10 W&O 1.3, 1.4; LRA 3.7, 11/12 LRA 3.1; W&O 1.1, 1.2; W 2.2
Materials needed: This worksheet.
Methodology: See below.

Why let someone else have your final words?

Write your own epitaph!

I. Identify the TONE of the epitaph you want your tombstone to have. Do you want it to be...

FUNNY
RELIGIOUS
CLEVER
SOMBER
HUMBLE
SCARY
SOMETHING ELSE?
(Hey, It's Your Choice!)

II. Identify the some of the most significant things for which you hope to be remembered?

1. _____ .
2. _____ .
3. _____ .
4. _____ .
5. _____ .

III. Now use the list to construct your own epitaph.

(Hey, have some fun. This doesn't necessarily mean it is what they are going to write when the time comes. Plus, by that time, are you really going to care?)

My Epitaph

_____
_____
_____
_____
_____
_____
_____

Figurative Language

Figurative language is deliberate exaggeration, when a speaker says something that they do NOT *literally* mean.

Traditionally, figurative language falls into a four specific categories:

HYPERBOLE
SIMILES
METAPHORS
&
PERSONIFICATION

- **Hyperbole** is a very strong exaggeration.
  Example: "He is stronger than ten giants."
    see page 20.

- A **simile** is a comparison between two objects using the words "like" or "as."
  Example: "She sings like a nightingale."
    see page 79.

- A **metaphor** is a comparison between two objects (without "like" or "as").
  Example: "Helen is an angel."
    see page 40.

- **Personification** gives an inhuman thing human qualities.
  Example: "The sunrise was jealous of her loveliness."
    see page 69.

Classic poets use figurative language:

> Come away, come away, death
> And in sad cypress let me be laid
> Fly away, fly away, breath;
> I am slain by a fair, cruel maid.
> *(Shakespeare)*

Hip-Hop poets use figurative language:

> I'm like the farmer, plantin words, people are seeds
> My truth is the soil; help you grow like trees.
> *(Nas)*

Haiku

CA Language Arts Standards Covered:
9/10 LRA 3.7; L&S 1.1; W&O 1.3, 1.4; 11/12 LRA 3.1; W&O 1.1, 1.2; W 2.2 R 2.0; LRA 3.4

Haiku presents a vivid picture and the poet's impression, sometimes with suggestions of spiritual insight. The traditional haiku is three lines long: the first line is five syllables, the second line is seven syllables, and the third line is five syllables.

BASHO was one of the most famous of all Haiku poets.

NOTE: In Japanese, the syllable count of the haikus below would be accurate. The English translation alters it.

An old pond!
A frog jumps in—
The sound of water.

•

No one travels
Along this way but I,
This autumn evening.

Modern Haiku's follow a syllabic structure (5,7,5). Haiku's are:

- Three lines long
  - The first line is five syllables
  - The second line is seven syllables
  - The third line is five syllables

For example:

What's in my headphones?
Nothing but Hip-Hop music,
Jay-Z, Tupac, Nas!

Poetry Writing Exercise: Write a Haiku

Have students construct their own haikus.

Give them the freedom to explore their own subject matters, but insist that they count out the syllables and follow the proper structure.

NOTE: For less advanced students have them literally count out the amount of syllables per line and write the number beside their work so to ensure accuracy.
For example:

What's in my headphones? (5)
Nothing but Hip-Hop music, (7)
Jay-Z, Tupac, Nas! (5)

Hyperbole
Interpretation Guide

CA Language Arts Standards Covered:
  9/10 R 1.1, 1.2, 2.2; LRA 3.7, 3.11; 11/12 LRA; 3.4; R 2.2

Hyperbole: A figure of speech that uses incredible exaggeration, or overstatement, for effect.

For example:

  I pulled up with a million trucks—lookin, smellin, feeling like a million bucks. *(Ludacris)*

People often use exaggeration to make their point strong and clear. In the example above, the speaker did not really have a million trucks; the speaker is boasting about his status as well as how good he feels. Most Hip-Hop lyrics contain a lot of hyperbole.

Hyperbole is commonly used in society. *For example:*

- I nearly died laughing.
- I knocked on the door a million times.
- John was so scared he jumped out of his skin.

Classic Poets use HYPERBOLE

  I love thee with the breath, smiles, tears
  of all my life!
  (Elizabeth Browning)

  This little world of mine has lost its light.
  (Dorothy Parker)

  A robin redbreast in a cage
  Sets all heaven in a rage.
  (William Blake)

Questions:

- In the first example does the poet *literally* love with her breath, smiles and tears?
- In the second example has the world *literally* lost its light?
- In the third example is ALL of heaven *literally* in a rage?

Hip-Hop Poets use HYPERBOLE

  A lot of MCs today really know how to please, but I gave birth to most of them MCs.
  (Roxanne Shante)
  My mom's words echo in my head and if I let go I'm dead.
  (Nas)
  I can roast an MC like a barbecue.
  (Big Daddy Kane)

Questions:

- In the first example did she *literally* give birth to them MCs?
- In the second example if the poet *literally* lets go will he die?
- In the third example will another rapper *literally* be put on a barbecue?

Poetry Writing Exercise: Hyperbole

Learning Objective: Students will identify and utilize the poetic device of hyperbole.
Standards Addressed: 9/10 W&O 1.3, 1.4; LRA 3.7, 3.11; 11/12 W&O 1.1, 1.2; W 2.2; LRA 3.4
Materials needed: This worksheet.
Methodology: See below.

Use the following writing prompts to create hyperbole.

I am so thirsty _____ .

The guy is so cheap _____ .

She is so smart _____ .

I love it more than _____ .

The teacher is so boring _____ .

A TALL TALE is a story that contains a great deal of exaggeration.

For example:

My grandfather came home from fishing yesterday and explained to me how he caught the largest bass in the river. But it wasn't just a gigantic bass — it was a gigantic, speaking bass. This is why, my grandfather explained, he didn't return home with the fish. The gigantic, speaking bass asked to be let go and my grandfather did as he was told.

Use hyperbole to create a TALL POEM. Your poem should:

- Tell a short story.
- Be filled with exaggeration.
- Be at least 8 lines long.
- Attempt to use a rhyme scheme.

For example:

Hip-Hop Star Hyperbole

        I'm the baddest rapper
            with the sweetest ride.
        But it's not about the money,
            it's about the pride.
        I came through with my army,
            my truck is like a tank.
        If you try to test me,
            I'll take you straight to the bank.

Hyperbole Poem

_____

_____

_____

_____

_____

_____

Illuminating Imagery – Classic

Harlem: A Dream Deferred

by Langston Hughes

What happens to a dream deferred?

Does it dry up
like a raisin in the sun
Or fester like a sore –
And then run?
Does it stink like rotten meat?
Or crust and sugar over –
Like a syrupy sweet?

Maybe it just sags
like a heavy load.

Or does it explode?

Illuminating Imagery – Classic
Interpretation Guide

CA Language Arts Standards Covered:
9/10 LRA 3.7, 3.11; L&S 1.1; W 2.2; W&O 1.3, 1.4; R 2.2; 11/12 W&O 1.1, 1.2; W 2.2; R 2.0; LRA 3.4

Imagery: The use of language to evoke a picture or a concrete sensation of a person, a thing, a place, or an experience.

Poetic Theme: Reach for Your Dreams

Identify how Hughes uses imagery for all five senses in his poem.

- *Sight:*   Does it dry up
  like a raisin in the sun
- *Taste:*   Or crust and sugar over –
  Like a syrupy sweet?
- *Touch:*   Maybe it just sags
  like a heavy load.
- *Smell:*   Does it stink like rotten meat?
- *Sound:*   Or does it explode?

How does the sum total of all of the imagery add up to answering the question put forth by the speaker in line one, "What happens to a dream deferred?"

Each image represents something that was once useful or productive but, having been left alone or unattended for too long (i.e., like a dream deferred), becomes useless, decayed and possibly even self-destructive.

- The raisin is dried up.
- The sore has festered and run (with infection and puss).
- The syrupy sweet is crusted and sugared over, too sweet to even taste appealing anymore.
- The meat has turned rotten and smells foul and disgusting.
- The dream itself has exploded, the sound of which is entirely destructive.

What is the unspoken message the speaker is telling the reader about going after their own dreams?

The speaker seems to be clearly saying that having dreams and not pursuing them will cause one to not only regret their not "going for it," but cause them to eventually crumble apart. It may be slow but at some point the stress, regrets and disappointment of NOT pursuing one's dreams will become too much and self-destruction will occur in some shape or form.

Illuminating Imagery – Classic
Student Worksheet

Imagery: The use of language to evoke a picture or a concrete sensation of a person, a thing, a place, or an experience.

Identify how Hughes uses imagery for all five senses in his poem.

- Sight: _____
  _____

- Taste: _____
  _____

- Touch: _____
  _____

- Smell: _____
  _____

- Sound: _____
  _____

How does the sum total of all of the imagery add up to answering the question put forth by the speaker in line one, "What happens to a dream deferred?"

_____
_____
_____
_____
_____

What is the unspoken message the speaker is telling the reader about going after their own dreams?

_____
_____
_____
_____
_____

Illuminating Imagery – Hip-Hop

Juicy

by Notorious B.I.G.

It was all a dream
I used to read Word Up magazine
Salt 'n Peppa and Heavy D up in the limousine
Hangin' pictures on my wall
5   Every Saturday Rap Attack, Mr. Magic, Marley Marl...

Now honies play me close like butter played toast
From the Mississippi down to the east coast...
Sold out seats to hear Biggie Smalls speak
Livin life without fear
10   Puttin' 5 karats in my baby girl's ears
Lunches, brunches, interviews by the pool
Considered a fool 'cause I dropped out of high school
Stereotypes of a black male misunderstood...

We used to fuss when the landlord dissed us
15   No heat, wonder why Christmas missed us
Birthdays was the worst days
Now we sip champagne when we thirsty
Uh, damn right I like the life I live
Cause I went from negative to positive
20   And it's all good...

Illuminating Imagery – Hip-Hop
Interpretation Guide

CA Language Arts Standards Covered:
9/10 LRA 3.7; L&S 1.1; W 2.2; W&O 1.3, 1.4; 11/12 W&O 1.1, 1.2; W 2.2;

Imagery: The use of language to evoke a picture or a concrete sensation of a person, a thing, a place, or an experience.

Poetic Theme: Reach for Your Dreams

NOTE: "Juicy" has been an anthem to the Hip-Hop community, much like "Harlem: A Dream Deferred" was to the Harlem Renaissance.

Line 16 claims that birthdays were the worst days? Why do you think the poet felt this way?

The poet most probably claims that birthdays were not a happy time because of his family's financial struggles. Most likely there weren't any presents or parties and instead of being a day of gladness, his birthday became an event filled with sorrow.

What images from the verse does the poet use to evoke images of the poverty he endured prior to achieving Hip-Hop fame?

- Lines 1–4: The poet speaks about how he used to only dream about being a famous celebrity, reading Hip-Hop magazines and staring at pictures of other famous Hip-Hop artists on his walls.
- Lines 12, 13: He boasts about how he was considered a fool because he did not fare well in school but he claims to simply have been misunderstood, not an idiot.
- Lines 14, 15: These lines provide the imagery for his some of his struggles with his landlord including no heat (and when one lives on the East Coast this can be a very big problem).
- Line 15: "Wonder why Christmas missed us" speaks to his early poverty.

What images from the verse does the poet use to evoke images of the rewards of wealth and Hip-Hop fame in the reader's mind?

- Line 6: "Now honies (i.e., girls) play me close like butter played toast" (meaning he gets a lot of ladies).
- Line 8: His concerts are sold out.
- Line 9: He no longer has to live in fear (of the ills of poverty).
- Line 10: "Puttin' 5 karats in my baby girl's ears" exemplifies how he is able to financially provide for his children in a way that his own parents could not.
- Line 17: "Now we sip champagne when we thirsty" showing how money is no longer an object in his life.

Essay Prompt

In Lines 18 & 19 the poet boasts how he turned a negative situation into a positive one. How can you do the same in your own life?

Answers will vary.

Illuminating Imagery – Hip-Hop
Student Worksheet

Imagery: The use of language to evoke a picture or a concrete sensation of a person, a thing, a place, or an experience.

Line 16 claims that birthdays were the worst days? Why do you think the poet felt this way?

_____

_____

_____

_____

_____

_____

What images from the verse does the poet use to evoke images of the poverty he endured prior to achieving Hip-Hop fame?

_____

_____

_____

_____

_____

What images from the verse does the poet use to evoke images of the rewards of wealth and Hip-Hop fame in the reader's mind?

_____

_____

_____

_____

ESSAY PROMPT: In Lines 18 & 19 the poet boasts how he turned a negative situation into a positive one. How can you do the same in your own life?

_____

_____

_____

_____

_____

Poetry Writing Exercise: Imagery

Learning Objective: Students will identify and utilize the poetic device of imagery.
Standards Addressed: 9/10 W&O 1.3, 1.4; LRA 3.7, 3.11; 11/12 W&O 1.1, 1.2; W 1.5, 2.2
Materials needed: This worksheet.
Methodology: See below.

1. **Have students create a column for each of their five senses with some blank space next to each sense they list.**

    For example:

    - *Touch:* _____
      _____

    - *Taste:* _____
      _____

    - *Smell:* _____
      _____

    - *Sight:* _____
      _____

    - *Sound:* _____
      _____

2. **Give each student a piece of paper with a different object written on it.**

    Have each student write down their perceptions of this object by filling in the blanks for their five senses. Encourage them to be vivid, abstract, colorful, literal — anything but boring!

3. **Have students create an additional line of description adding the sixth component of emotion.**

    How do they feel about the object? Does it remind them of something (like a relative, a special time in their childhood or a location they once visited)?

4. **Have students use their work (above) as material to write a poem about their object.**

    Allow them the freedom to make it as long (or short) as they wish, using rhyme, free verse, personification (teacher's discretion) but stress the importance of using all of the material above in their work.

5. **Have students give their poem a title.**

    For example: Object Poem (Light Bulb)

Just Give Me the Light

Smooth is my bulb
Tastes like hot electricity
Smells like smokey possibility
Ruler of Light
Gives my home sight
Sound like a buzz
we shut off every night.

Detecting Irony

The Fish

by Elizabeth Bishop

1   I caught a tremendous fish
     and held him beside the boat
     half out of water, with my hook
     fast in a corner of its mouth.
5   He didn't fight.
     He hadn't fought at all.

Detecting Irony
Interpretation Guide

CA Language Arts Standards Covered:
9/10 LRA 3.4, 3.7, 3.8; L&S 1.1; W 2.2; W&O 1.3, 1.4; R 2.2 11/12 LRA 3.3, 3.4; W&O 1.1, 1.2; W 2.2; R 2.0

Irony: In general, it is the difference between the way something appears and what is actually true.

What makes lines 5 and 6 ironic in the poem?

Lines 5 and 6 are ironic because the speaker claims to have caught "a tremendous fish" which one would assume would put up a "tremendous" fight. Since the fish appears one way (i.e., tremendous) yet actually acts another (i.e., it acts very non-tremendously) the situation could be interpreted as being ironical.

VERBAL IRONY is irony that is spoken aloud.
(Sarcasm is a form of verbal irony).
We see it all around us every day.

Read the conversation below between a couple that is on the verge of getting a divorce and can't stand the sight of one another. Their words are filled with VERBAL IRONY.

Wife: "Hi, it's so nice to see you."

Husband: "Wow, you look good in that dress. Putting on those extra pounds really fills you out in a complimentary manner."

Wife: "Well, I just love your hair. That toupee is smashing. But I have to admit, your previous baldness was quite sexy."

Why could the wife's first line be considered ironic?

This is ironic because, if the couple really can't stand the sight of one another and is about to get a divorce, the wife probably HATES seeing her husband.

Why could the husband's response be considered ironic?

The husband's response could be considered ironic (or sarcastic) because he is not really complimenting her physical looks — he is telling her she looks fat, which is most likely something he knows will get his soon-to-be ex-wife very angry.

Why could the wife's response be considered ironic?

The wife's response may be considered ironic (or sarcastic) because she has fired back to insult the husband by ridiculing his fake hair and teasing him about his baldness.

Detecting Irony
Student worksheet

Irony: In general, it is the difference between the way something appears and what is actually true.

What makes lines 5 and 6 ironic in the poem?

_____

_____

_____

_____

VERBAL IRONY is irony that is spoken aloud.
(Sarcasm is a form of verbal irony).

Read the conversation below between a couple that is on the verge of getting a divorce and can't stand the sight of one other. Their words are filled with VERBAL IRONY.

Wife: "Hi, it's so nice to see you."

Husband: "Wow, you look good in that dress. Putting on those extra pounds really fills you out in a complimentary manner."

Wife: "Well, I just love your hair. That toupee is smashing. But I have to admit, your previous baldness was quite sexy."

Why could the wife's first line be considered ironic?

_____

_____

Why could the husband's response be considered ironic?

_____

_____

_____

_____

_____

Why could the wife's response be considered ironic?

_____

_____

_____

_____

Unearthing Meaning – Classic

Do Not Go Gentle into That Good Night

by Dylan Thomas

Do not go gentle into that good night,
Old age should burn and rave at close of day;
Rage, rage against the dying of the light.

Though wise men at their end know dark is right,
Because their words had forked no lightning they
Do not go gentle into that good night.

Good men, the last wave by, crying how bright
Their frail deeds might have danced in a green bay,
Rage, rage against the dying of the light.

Wild men who caught and sang the sun in flight,
And learn, too late, they grieved it on its way,
Do not go gentle into that good night.

Grave men, near death, who see with blinding sight
Blind eyes could blaze like meteors and be gay,
Rage, rage against the dying of the light.

And you, my father, there on the sad height,
Curse, bless, me now with your fierce tears, I pray.
Do not go gentle into that good night.
Rage, rage against the dying of the light.

Unearthing Meaning – Classic
Interpretation Guide

CA Language Arts Standards Covered:
9/10 LRA 3.7; L&S 1.1; W 2.2; W&O 1.3, 1.4; R 2.2 11/12 W&O 1.1, 1.2; W 2.2; R 2.0, 2.2, 2.4, 2.5; LRA 3.2, 3.3, 3.4

Meaning: What is the poem about?

Poetic Theme: Fight for Survival

What is the essential, overall "meaning" of Dylan Thomas's poem?

The poem basically urges people, "Not to give up easily." Though death is inevitable, and it is part of the natural cycle of life, people need to fight, claw, scrape and do whatever must be done to stay alive—especially in the face of impending death.

How does the poetic tool of repetition emphasize meaning in Thomas's poem?

The repetition of two specific lines: "Do no go gentle into that good night" and "Rage, rage against the dying of the light" basically urges people, "Not to give up easily." The repetition of these lines almost INSISTS that the fight for life be continued despite any hurdles one may be forced to face.

To illuminate the meaning, paraphrase what the line, "Do no go gentle into that good night" is really saying.

In the line, "Do no go gentle into that good night," night is a metaphor for death and dying. The speaker of the poem is urging people not to "go gentle" (i.e., passively follow along) into death's arms, but rather fight for life.

To illuminate the meaning, paraphrase what the line, "Rage, rage against the dying of the light" is really saying.

In the line, "Rage, rage against the dying of the light," the phrase dying of the light is also a metaphor for the end of life. By using the strong action verb "Rage", the speaker of the poem is insisting, almost commanding, that death is not something to be passively accepted but rather, to be passionately and viciously fought against with every last bit of strength and energy.

What are the unspoken beliefs about life that you believe the speaker of the poem holds?

Life is a precious gift and one must wring out every drip and drop of it, as if from a sponge, before they die. Not to do so is not to live life fully and makes death a sad event. Doing so allows for one to find that eventual "good night", a metaphor for a peaceful afterlife.

Unearthing Meaning – Classic
Student worksheet

Meaning: What is the poem about?

What is the essential, overall "meaning" of Dylan Thomas's poem?

_____

_____

_____

_____

How does the poetic tool of repetition emphasize meaning in Thomas's poem?

_____

_____

_____

_____

To illuminate the meaning, paraphrase what the line, "Do no go gentle into that good night" is really saying.

_____

_____

_____

_____

To illuminate the meaning, paraphrase what the line, "Rage, rage against the dying of the light" is really saying.

_____

_____

_____

_____

What are the unspoken beliefs about life that you believe the speaker of the poem holds?

_____

_____

_____

_____

Unearthing Meaning – Hip-Hop

Me Against the World

By Tupac Shakur (2Pac)

1   With all this extra stressin'
The question I wonder is, after death, after my last breath
When will I finally get to rest? Through this suppression
They punish the people that's askin' questions
5   And those that possess, steal from the ones without possessions
The message I stress: to make it stop, study your lessons
Don't settle for less—even the genius asks questions
Be grateful for your blessings
Don't ever change, keep your essence
10   The power is in the people and the politics we address
Always do your best, don't let the pressure make you panic
And when you get stranded
And things don't go the way you planned it
Dreamin' of riches, in a position of makin' a difference
15   Politicians and hypocrites, they don't wanna listen
If I'm insane, it's the fame made a brother change
It wasn't nothing like the game
It's just me against the world

Unearthing Meaning – Hip-Hop
Interpretation Guide

CA Language Arts Standards Covered:
9/10 LRA 3.7; L&S 1.1; R 3.0 W 2.2; W&O 1.3, 1.4; 11/12 W&O 1.1, 1.2; W 2.2; R 2.5, 3.0; LRA 3.2, 3.4

Meaning: What is the poem about?

Poetic Theme: *Fight for Survival*

What is the essential, overall "meaning" in Tupac's lyrics?

In a very straightforward manner, the poet's meaning is explained in the title. (It is him against the world.) On a wider basis, the poet is speaking metaphorically to people who share the same plight in life that the poet does (i.e., socioeconomically disadvantaged minorities in the U.S.). As a result it is "them" against the world as well.

Explain the forces that create a "Me against the world" situation in the poem?

Injustice has created a "Me Against the World" mentality in the poem. The poet addresses sources of injustice in our society by pointing out that it is often the people who are "askin' questions" that are punished (Lines 4 & 5).
(**NOTE:** Historically, political instigators have been scrutinized and penalized for questioning authority. From Voltaire to Mandela, this is true.) The poet also addresses the issues of the "haves and the have-nots" in the classical reference of the rich taking from the poor (Line 5).

How does Tupac suggest we overcome oppression?

In Lines 6 & 7, Tupac stresses the importance of understanding history ("Study your lessons") and asking questions ("even the genius asks questions"). Basically, the poet shows how knowledge is the tool by which oppression is overcome.
In Line 10, Tupac further highlights ways of addressing power and politics through getting people to recognize that power lies in their hands.

If the poet's circumstances are so dire and life has so much injustice, explain why the poet would tell the reader to "Be grateful for your blessings" – Lines 8?

The poet readily admits he has had a hard life (it is a common theme in Tupac's work—see *Dear Mama*), but he stresses the value in adversity because it makes one stronger. By being grateful, one removes themselves from the destructive forces of self-pity so they can find a positive way to change their circumstances. The poet is not just pointing out the negatives of injustice in this work, but giving positive insights as to ways to overcome them in life.

Explain the meaning of why the poet insists the listener should not "ever change/keep your essence" – Line 9.

Tupac Shakur strived to stay true to his ideals throughout his life and a common theme in his music (and this poem) is that people should stay true to their hearts, their cultures and their politics. Essentially, this poem is a cautionary warning against all the different forces that someone who tries to stay true to their beliefs is going to run up against (i.e., riches, hypocrites, politicians, power, etc. ...). Yet Tupac, as the voice of experience, implores the reader to hold true to their core values.

Unearthing Meaning – Hip-Hop
Student Worksheet

Meaning: What is the poem about?

What is the essential, overall "meaning" of Tupac's lyrics?

_____

_____

_____

_____

Explain the forces that create a "Me against the world" situation in the poem?

_____

_____

_____

_____

How does Tupac suggest we overcome oppression?

_____

_____

_____

_____

If the poet's circumstances are so dire and life has so much injustice, explain why the poet would tell the reader to "Be grateful for your blessings" – Lines 8?

_____

_____

_____

_____

Explain the meaning of why the poet insists the listener should not "ever change/keep your essence" – Line 9.

_____

_____

_____

_____

_____

_____

_____

_____

Unearthing Meaning
Activities

CA Language Arts Standards Covered:
    9/10 W&O 1.3, 1.4; L&S 2.4 LRA 3.2, 3.5, 3.7, 3.12 11/12 W&O 1.1, 1.2; W 2.2; LRA 3.2

COMPARE AND CONTRAST: *Classic Poetry to Hip-Hop*

For Classroom Discussion or Writing Prompt

1. **Have students explain the common beliefs they feel that Dylan Thomas and Tupac Shakur share about life?**

    ANSWERS WILL VARY but some possible points mentioned will be...

   • Life is precious.
   • One must follow their heart.
   • Death is not something to fear but its inevitable presence should make us realize the need to bravely dare to reach for our dreams. There are things worth fighting for in life.

2. **Do you feel that the work of contemporary Hip-Hop poets in general get the positive recognition they deserve? Why or why not?**

    ANSWERS WILL VARY but some possible points mentioned will be...

   No, Hip-Hop poets are NOT recognized for their skill and literary merit. Hip-Hop poets are considered "shallow" due to misperceptions by larger society. These misperceptions include that Hip-Hop is solely filled with "Gangstas," that Hip-Hop poets are not intelligent and that Hip-Hop poets are not aware/do not understand the works of "classic poets." All of these are untrue.

Poetry Writing Exercise: Meaning

Learning Objective: Students will recognize and create a poem with personal meaning using introspective reflection.
Standards Addressed: 9/10 W&O 1.3, 1.4; LRA 3.7, 11/12 W&O 1.1, 1.2
Materials needed: This worksheet.
Methodology: Create an "I am" poem. (See below.)

Fill in the blanks:

I am _____

    (two special characteristics)

I am _____

    (something you are actually curious about)

I am _____

    (an imaginary sound)

I am _____

    (an imaginary sight)

I am _____

    (an actual desire)

I am _____

    (something that makes you very sad)

I am _____

    (something you love)

I am _____

    (what are you?)

Rewrite your poem using your sentence and adding a description.

For example:

I Am	*I Am*
I am smart and athletic,	_____
an athlete and a scholar.	
I am the world, a colorful map.	_____
I am a swish, the perfection of flight.	_____
I am the color behind your eyes,	_____
dark and light.	
I am a good meal, hearty and healthy.	_____
I am a baby's tears, the pain of longing.	_____
I am the laughter of friends, in the morning.	_____
I am me!	_____
	by_____

Making Meaning of Metaphors – Classic

The Weaver

by Anonymous

My life is but a weaving, between my God and me,
I do not choose the colors, He worketh steadily.
Ofttimes he weaveth sorrow, and I in foolish pride
Forget He sees the upper, and I the underside.
Not till the loom is silent, and the shuttles cease to fly,
Will God unroll the canvas, and explain the reasons why
The dark threads are as needful in the skillful weaver's hand
As threads of gold and silver in the pattern He has planned.

He knows, He loves, He cares,
Nothing this truth can dim.
He gives His very best to those
Who leave the choice with Him.

Making Meaning of Metaphors – Classic
Interpretation Guide

CA Language Arts Standards Covered:
9/10 LRA 3.7, 3.11; L&S 1.1; W 2.2; R 1.1, 1.2, W&O 1.3, 1.4; R 2.2 11/12 W&O 1.1, 1.2; LRA 3.4; W 2.2; R 2.0

Metaphor: A figure of speech that makes a comparison between two unlike things **without** the use of **like** or **as.**

For example:

Education is a life raft in the ocean of the American job market.

Poetic Theme: God's Influence on Life

Identify and explain the two, main, unlike things being compared in the poem that are being used as metaphors which the speaker uses to make sense of his life.

The speaker uses two metaphors to make sense of his life. The first metaphor is that his life is a weaving, like a carpet or a quilt or a blanket. Since life and blankets are two uncommon things to compare with one another, this is a good metaphor because it is original and new.

The second metaphor the speaker uses is that God is the weaver (that's where the title comes from). God is the one who works the loom (i.e., creates the patterns, chooses the colors, determines the direction). Since God and weavers are two uncommon things to compare with one another, this is also a good metaphor because it is original and new.

Good metaphors put very clear and memorable pictures inside of the reader's head. What picture does the poem give of the blanket that is his life?

The blanket has colors, with some threads of gold and silver in the pattern. These could be interpreted as symbols of the good things that life has to offer. Not necessarily "wealth" or financial "riches" either. They could be loved ones, family, friends, good health, fulfilling work, great neighbors, etc. … There seem to be many things (i.e., colors) that the speaker finds which are positive in life.

The blanket also has its "dark threads" (Line 7). The speaker points them out as being "needful to the skillful weaver." Dark colors provide a contrast by which the "light colors" can be better seen/ appreciated. This idea can be interpreted as we need to have some sadness in our lives in order to better appreciate the good things we have.

What picture does the speaker give of God as the weaver of the speaker's life?

The speaker draws a picture of God as a master weaver, with a full palette of colors and threads from which to choose in order to weave the blanket that he wishes. Though the speaker sometimes fails to understand the choices God makes—such as sorrow or sadness or loss being woven into the fabric of life—the speaker basically says that only the master weaver can understand the master plan. This is because only he can see "the upper, and I the underside" (line 4).

Basically, who can ever know what direction the master plan for the entire carpet (or for one's entire life)? The answer is God and only God (i.e., the weaver) and therefore, judging events before one can see how they fit into the whole scheme of life is not really practical or doable. All must be taken in the scope of entirety and wholeness.

The final stanza goes on to reassure us that the weaver "know, cares and loves us" and that it all works out best for those who trust the weaver.

Making Meaning of Metaphors – Classic
Student Worksheet

Metaphor: A figure of speech that makes a comparison between two unlike things **without** the use of **like** or **as.**

For example:

Education is a life raft in the ocean of the American job market.

Identify and explain the two, main, unlike things being compared in the poem that are being used as metaphors which the speaker uses to make sense of his life.

_____

_____

_____

_____

_____

_____

Good metaphors put very clear and memorable pictures inside of the reader's head. What picture does the poem give of the blanket that is his life?

_____

_____

_____

_____

_____

_____

What picture does the speaker give of God as the weaver of the speaker's life?

_____

_____

_____

_____

_____

_____

_____

Making Meaning of Metaphor – Hip-Hop

Respiration

by Mos Def

1   The new moon rode high in the crown of the metropolis
      Shinin', like who one top of this?
      People was tusslin', arguin' and bustlin'
      Gangstaz of Gotham hardcore hustlin'…
      The cops and the robbers, they both partners, they all heartless
5   With no conscience, back streets stay darkened
      Where unbeliever hearts stay hardened…
      Like city lights stay throbbin'
      You either make a way or stay sobbin', the shiny apple
      Is bruised but sweet and if you choose to eat
10   You could lose your teeth, many crews retreat
      Nightly news repeat, who got shot down and locked down
      Spotlight to savages, NADSDAQ averages
      My narrative, rose to explain this existence
      Amidst the harbor lights which remain in the distance

15   So much on my mind that I can't recline
      Blastin' holes in the night till she bled sunshine
      Breathe in, inhale vapors from bright stars that shine
      Breathe out, we smoke retrace the skyline
      Heard the bass ride out like an ancient mating call
20   I can't take it y'all, I can feel the city breathin'
      Chest heavin', against the flesh of the evening
      Sigh before we die like the last train leavin'…

Making Meaning of Metaphors – Hip-Hop
Interpretation Guide

CA Language Arts Standards Covered:
9/10 LRA 3.7, 3.11; L&S 1.1; R 1.1, 1.2; W 2.2; W&O 1.3, 1.4; 11/12 W&O 1.1, 1.2; W 2.2; LRA 3.4

Metaphor: A figure of speech that makes a comparison between two unlike things **without** the use of **like** or **as.**

For example:

Education is a life raft in the ocean of the American job market.

Poetic Theme: The City's Influence on Life

Identify the central metaphor in the verse and explain how the two unlike things are being compared to one another to illustrate the speaker's point.

The central metaphor that is being used in the poem is a city that is being compared to a person. Although the city is filled with people and life, it also metaphorically has its own life.

- Line 1: the moon rises high "in the crown of the metropolis."
  This "crowning" gives the city a sense of having a head to be crowned, like a noble king.
- Line 16: "the night bled sunshine" is a metaphor for the sunrise using the human quality of bleeding to descriptively illustrate the point.
- Line 20, 21 & 22: the city is "breathin'," the city has a heaving chest, the evening is given flesh and the last train "sighs" as if it were a person.

Good metaphors put very clear and memorable pictures in the reader's head.
What picture is given in Lines 8-10, and what do these pictures stand for metaphorically?

The image portrayed in lines 8-10 is of a bruised and shiny apple, which has been given the qualities of sweetness but also has the ability to "make you lose your teeth."

Metaphorically, the apple represents New York City (a.k.a. "the Big Apple"). New York can be sweet (some of the finest culture in the world exists in NYC) but it can also be dangerous. The line "you could lose your teeth" is a direct reference to the notorious violence in NYC and there have even been instances where people have literally had their teeth knocked out and stolen (i.e., gold capped teeth popular with urban youth).

Explain how you believe the speaker of the poem feels about New York City. Why?

The speaker has mixed emotions about NYC. On one hand, the poet's tone shows affection for New York, born of great appreciation and respect. After all, the city is crowned like a king to open the poem and the audience gets the sense that the city is held in great favor, much like anyone else might look upon their hometown with fondness.

On the other hand, the speaker is not afraid to frankly address the huge injustices, problems and wrongs that also have a home in New York. References to the omnipresent violence and danger, a lack of conscience on behalf of both criminals and cops and the existence of savages, gunshots and incarcerations demonstrate this. Overall, the speaker has a love/hate relationship with NYC but one gets the sense he would not trade NYC for any other place on earth.

Making Meaning of Metaphor – Hip-Hop
Student Worksheet

Metaphor: A figure of speech that makes a comparison between two unlike things **without** the use of **like** or **as.**

For example:

Education is a life raft in the ocean of the American job market.

Identify the central metaphor in the verse and explain how the two unlike things are being compared to one another to illustrate the speaker's point.

_____
_____
_____
_____
_____
_____

Good metaphors put very clear and memorable pictures in the reader's head. What picture is given in Lines 8-10, and what do these pictures stand for metaphorically?

_____
_____
_____
_____
_____
_____

Explain how you believe the speaker of the poem feels about New York City. Why?

_____
_____
_____
_____
_____
_____

Poetry Writing Exercise: Metaphor

Learning Objective: Students will identify and utilize the poetic device of metaphor.
Standards Addressed: 9/10 W&O 1.3, 1.4; LRA 3.7, 3.11; R 1.1, 1.2 11/12 LRA 3.4; W&O 1.1, 1.2; W 2.2
Materials needed: This worksheet.
Methodology: See below.

Create 3 metaphors comparing the universe to an object.

*For example: The sun **is a light bulb.***

1. _____ .
2. _____ .
3. _____ .

Create 3 metaphors comparing an emotion to an object.

*For example: Sadness **is a vacuum.***

1. _____ .
2. _____ .
3. _____ .

Create 3 metaphors comparing a person to an object.

*For example: My father **is a dictionary.***

1. _____ .
2. _____ .
3. _____ .

Write a poem using at least 3 metaphors comparing something important to you to how you feel about it.

For example:

Music Metaphor Poem	*Metaphor Poem*
Music is a joy	_____
Filling my heart with beats	_____
Music is a flame	_____
Filling my ears with heat	_____
Music is my soul	_____
Music makes me whole	_____
	by_____

Grasping Mood – Classic

We Real Cool

by Gwendolyn Brooks

> We real cool. We
> Left school. We
>
> Lurk late. We
> Strike straight. We
>
> Sing sin. We
> Thin gin. We
>
> Jazz June. We
> Die soon.

Grasping Mood – Classic
Interpretation Guide

CA Language Arts Standards Covered:
9/10 LRA 3.4, 3.7, L&S 1.1; W 2.2; W&O 1.3, 1.4 11/12 LRA 3.2, 3.3, 3.4; W&O 1.1, 1.2; W 2.2; R 2.0, 2.2, 2.4, 2.5

Mood: The feeling created in the reader by the poem or story.

Poetic Theme: Adolescence

Describe the physical location where you feel this poem most likely takes place.

This poem has a sense of taking place in a smoky bar or a pool hall or some other sort of club where "bad boys (and girls)" traditionally hang out.

Explain which lines from the poem support your beliefs about this physical location.

- It's a place where "cool" people hang out (Line 1).
- It's not school (Line 2). As a matter of fact, it is most likely a location where people who traditionally don't favor school like to spend their time.
- It's also a place where people "lurk late" (Line 3), "Sin" (Line 5), drink "gin" (Line 6), hear "jazz" (Line 7), and apparently, "die" young (Line 8).

Who do you think are the speakers of the poem (who are the "we")? Explain why?

The "we" in the poem appear to be a group of teenagers, sort of "bad boy" types though there could be a few "tough chicks" mixed in with their group as well. The reasons for this are similar to the reasons cited above regarding the physical location of the poem.

- The "We" are "cool" (Line 1).
- The "We" "lurk late" (Line 3). Notice how they don't just hang out, but lurk, a sinister sounding word.
- The "We" "Sin" (Line 5) and drink "gin" (Line 6) and listen to "jazz" (Line 7) with an almost defiant sense of glee.

*Considering what you have deduced about the location and people, what is the overall feeling (i.e., the **mood**) created in the reader by the work? Explain why you feel this way.*

At first, the mood of the poem is enticing and alluring. The "we" in the poem are appealing because they are "cool". They hold the same sort of appeal a band of renegades or pirates does. They are dangerous yet their danger makes them interesting and attractive. They are proud to proclaim that they hang out late, drink, sin and play by their own rules (much like the musical art form of jazz). And they don't make any apologies for their lifestyle.

But the mood of the poem changes very abruptly in the last line "Die soon". The poem's feeling suddenly shifts from bloated pride to hollow emptiness. There is an element of stark finality to the last line, which has been created in two ways. First, it comes from the pattern being broken. The word "We" had been repeated over and over as the last line of each of the previous seven lines in the poem. As a reader, we came to expect another "We." After the words "Die soon" there is no more "We" almost as if to say, we all die alone. When this "We" does not come readers are left with the sudden realization that not only is the word "We" not coming, but nothing else is coming either.

The poem has ended... abruptly. In addition, the sense of death, which has suddenly entered the poem, completely turns the whole mood of the work from one of proud defiance to one of stark nothingness. There is nothing cool about dying. It is not made glamorous, the tone is not boastful (like the other lines) and there is almost a cautionary sense about the whole lifestyle of the people in the poem that is suddenly illuminated. The poem seems to be saying that if you live like "we" do, an early death is almost imminent. The poem's sudden mood shift also seems to indicate that dying in this manner is starkly tragic.

Grasping Mood – Classic
Student Worksheet

Mood: The feeling created in the reader by the poem or story.

Describe the physical location where you feel this poem most likely takes place.

_____

_____

_____

_____

_____

Explain which lines from the poem support your beliefs about this physical location.

_____

_____

_____

_____

_____

Who do you think are the speakers of the poem? In other words, who are the "we"?
Explain why you feel this to be the case.

_____

_____

_____

_____

_____

Considering what you have deduced about the location and the people in the poem,
what is the overall feeling (i.e., the **mood***) created in the reader by the work?*
Explain why you feel this way.

_____

_____

_____

_____

_____

Grasping Mood – Hip-Hop

(A LIGHT MOOD POEM)

A Roller Skating Jam Named "Saturdays"

by De La Soul, verse by Dove

1   Oh Mr. Sprinkler, Mr. Sprinkler
    Wet me for one, Mr. Sprinkler
    I'm heatin' high-five in a daze, no split
    With a yawn I trip to the dawn
5   Out comes the bodies following the one idea
    It's clear, rattle to the roll
    Hold back up the track, grab your roller skates y'all
    And let's zip on by
    Zip-a-de-doo-dah, let's zip on by.
10   Sun is on thick and the cheese is rollin' quick
    Come on, there's no time to hide
    Season is twist, spinning and winning
    No hackey sack, let me in
    Spill on the bottom away, but it's okay, huh
15   It's a Saturday

(A DARK MOOD POEM)

Follow Me

by Sage Francis

1   The secretive type
    I like to creep in the night
    When you hear me speaking under my breath to be polite
    (I'm talking about you)
5   Inconspicuous, keep killing that sweet feeling
    The mystique's building
    I only speak to the freakishly chic children

Grasping Mood – Hip-Hop
Interpretation Guide

CA Language Arts Standards Covered:
9/10 LRA 3.7, 3.9; L&S 1.1; W 2.2; W&O 1.3, 1.4; R 2.2; 11/12 W&O 1.1, 1.2; W 2.2; R 2.0; LRA 3.3, 3.4

Mood: The feeling created in the reader by the poem or story.

Poetic Theme: Adolescence
A Roller Skating Jam Named "Saturdays"
by De La Soul, verse by Dove

Describe the physical location where you feel De La Soul poem most likely takes place. Explain which lines support your beliefs about this physical location.

The De La Soul poem gives the reader the sense that activities are taking place outdoors on a hot, summer Saturday. (Saturday comes from the both the title itself and Line 15.) The "Sun is on thick" (Line 10) directly references the "heat" of the day. (When something is "thick," there is a lot of it.) Basically, the speaker wakes up, grabs his roller skates and goes off to "Zip-a-de-doo-dah, let's zip on by" (Line 9).

What is the overall feeling/mood created in the reader by the work? Explain why you feel this way.

The mood of these lyrics conveys excitement and happiness for the beautiful day to come. As it says in Line 5, the "bodies" all come out to follow the "one idea" (which is to roller skate with friends and enjoy the day). The author has given the passage whimsical qualities by the choice of words (Line 9, "rattle to the roll" has a playful quality) and his use of onomatopoeia (Line 9, "Zip-a-de-doo-dah" reference) makes it even that much more lighthearted. In Line 12, people are "spinning" and the "season is twist." These lines all enhance the lively, upbeat, and fun mood of the verse. Finally in Line 14, the writer even takes a spill (i.e., crashes), but no worries because… "But it's ok, huh/It's a Saturday" (Lines 14, 15).

Follow Me
by Sage Francis

Describe the location where you feel Francis's poem takes place. Support your beliefs.

This poem appears to take place in an urban environment. Secretive dealings (Line 1) creeping in the night (Line 2) while speaking under one's breath (Line 3) suggest back alleys, dark hallways and lots of shadowy corners and tall buildings.

What is the overall feeling/ mood created in the reader by the work? Support your beliefs.

The mood is ominous and dark. It appears to be a place of danger, mystery and covert dealings. This is created through the vocabulary of words such as freakishly (Line 7), mystique (Line 6), and the alliteration and word choice in the phrase "keep killing" (Line 5).

Grasping Mood – Hip-Hop
Student Worksheet

Mood: The feeling created in the reader by the poem or story.

A Roller Skating Jam Named "Saturdays"

by De La Soul, verse by Dove

Describe the physical location where you feel De La Soul poem most likely takes place. Explain which lines support your beliefs about this physical location.

_____

_____

_____

_____

What is the overall feeling/mood created in the reader by the work? Explain why you feel this way.

_____

_____

_____

_____

Follow Me

by Sage Francis

Describe the location where you feel Francis's poem takes place. Please support your beliefs.

_____

_____

_____

_____

What is the overall feeling/mood created in the reader by the work? Please support your beliefs.

_____

_____

_____

_____

Poetry Writing Exercise: Mood

Learning Objective: Students will identify and utilize the poetic device of mood.
Standards Addressed: 9/10 W&O 1.3, 1.4; LRA 3.7, 11/12 W&O 1.1, 1.2; W 1.5, 2.2
Materials needed: This worksheet.
Methodology: See below.

List three descriptive words or phrases that define the following:

For example:

    Striking out (baseball)   1. shame   2. slump   3. gut-wrenching

- A dark alley   1. _____   2. _____   3. _____
- A Sunday picnic   1. _____   2. _____   3. _____
- Valentine's Day   1. _____   2. _____   3. _____
- The Principal's Office   1. _____   2. _____   3. _____
- A stray dog   1. _____   2. _____   3. _____

Create a MOOD POEM:

1. **Determine the subject of the poem. (You may use the list... or not.)**

2. **Determine the mood you wish to create in the poem.**

3. **Choose an appropriate setting for the poem.**

4. **Use vivid language to craft a specific "feel."**

   For example:

       Striking out (baseball)   1. shame   2. slump   3. gut-wrenching

Striking Out

All eyes are on the last batter
Da-duump! A heartbeat.
The hot sun — unforgiving
As STRIKE THREE!!!
Slumping back to the bench,
Watching victors
head for the ice cream truck.
His stomach in knots
No taste for sweets.

Mood Poem

_____

_____

_____

_____

_____

_____

_____

Onomatopoeia: A Funny Word, Descriptive Sounds – Classic

The Congo

by Vachel Lindsay

1   Their Basic Savagery
    Fat black bucks in a wine-barrel room,
    Barrel-house kings, with feet unstable,
    Sagged and reeled and pounded on the table,
5   Pounded on the table,
    Beat an empty barrel with the handle of a broom,
    Hard as they were able,
    Boom, boom, Boom,
    With a silk umbrella and the handle of a broom,
10   Boomlay, boomlay, boomlay, Boom.

    THEN I had religion. THEN I had a vision.
    I could not turn from their revel in derision.
    THEN I SAW THE CONGO, CREEPING THROUGH THE BLACK,
    CUTTING THROUGH THE JUNGLE WITH A GOLDEN TRACK.
15   Then along that river-bank
    A thousand miles
    Tattoed cannibals danced in files;
    Then I heard the boom of the blood-lust song
    And a thigh-bone beating on a tin-pan gong.
20   And "BLOOD" screamed the whistles and the fifes of the warriors,
    "BLOOD" screamed the skull-faced, lean witch-doctors,
    "Whirl ye the deadly voodoo rattle,
    Harry the uplands,
    Steal all the cattle,
25   Rattle-rattle, rattle-rattle,
    Bing!
    Boomlay, boomlay, boomlay, Boom,"
    A roaring, epic, rag-time tune
    From the mouth of the Congo
30   To the Mountains of the Moon.
    Death is an Elephant,
    Torch-eyed and horrible,
    Foam-flanked and terrible.
    Boom, …
35   Boom, …
    Boom, …
    Like the wind
    Hoo, Hoo, Hoo.

Onomatopoeia: A Funny Word, Descriptive Sounds – Classic
Interpretation Guide

CA Language Arts Standards Covered:
   9/10 LRA 3.2, 3.7, 3.9, 3.12; L&S 1.1, 1.11; W 2.2; W&O 1.3, 1.4;
   R 2.2 11/12 W&O 1.1, 1.2; W 2.2; R 2.0, 2.5; LRA 3.4

Onomatopoeia: The use of a word whose sound imitates or suggests its meaning.

For example:

   Boom! Smash! Pow! Pssst. Ssshh!

Identify at least three lines where the poet uses the technique of onomatopoeia in the poem "The Congo".

- Line 8   Boom, boom, Boom
- Line 25   Rattle-rattle, Rattle-rattle
- Line 38   Hoo, Hoo, Hoo

Explain what effect the use of onomatopoeia creates in the poem?

Using onomatopoeia creates vividness and sensory imagery in the poem in a unique and striking manner. Words like *Boom, Bing, Boomlay* and *Hoo* virtually bring the audience directly into the Congo.

Onomatopoeia, when used this way, can be an incredibly effective force for creating feeling in poetry. Using onomatopoeia, such as the poet has, exemplifies how imitating the sounds associated with the objects or actions of an experience can having a drastic and exciting effect.

Describe 3 people in "The Congo" and match the poet's use of onomatopoeia to describing these people and their actions. (Please cite specific line numbers.)

Three types of people who live in the Congo for which the poet uses onomatopoeia to describe are:
- Savages who pound empty barrels (*Boom* – Line 6)
- Witch doctors who draw on voodoo (*Rattle* – Line 25)
- Tattooed Cannibals who sing blood lust songs (*Boomlay* – Line 27)

CONTROVERSIAL ISSUE

Class Discussion or Writing Prompt

This poem has been referred to as "a legitimate variety of Negro dialect" by some scholars of poetry. Others scholars of poetry have called the author "racist" due to his portrayal of Africans in the work because the author of the poem is "white" and the people described in the poem are not just "black," but negative stereotypes of Africans (i.e., savages beating drums, tattooed cannibals, witch doctors, etc.)

Which opinion do you agree with? Why?

Answers will vary.

Onomatopoeia: A Funny Word, Descriptive Sounds – Classic
Student Worksheet

Onomatopoeia: The use of a word whose sound imitates or suggests its meaning.

For example:

Boom! Smash! Pow! Pssst. Ssshh!

Identify at least three lines where the poet uses the technique of onomatopoeia in the poem "The Congo".

_____

_____

_____

_____

Explain what effect the use of onomatopoeia creates in the poem?

_____

_____

_____

_____

Describe 3 people in "The Congo" and match the poet's use of onomatopoeia to describing these people and their actions. (Please cite specific line numbers.)

_____

_____

_____

_____

_____

CONTROVERSIAL ISSUE

This poem has been referred to as "a legitimate variety of Negro dialect" by some scholars of poetry. Others scholars of poetry have called the author "racist" due to his portrayal of Africans in the work because the author of the poem is "white" and the people described in the poem are not just "black," but negative stereotypes of Africans (i.e., savages beating drums, tattooed cannibals, witch doctors, etc.).

With which opinion do you agree? Why?

_____

_____

_____

_____

Onomatopoeia: A Funny Word, Descriptive Sounds – Hip-Hop

Datskat

by The Roots

1   Di-bi-dis-banks, hip-flip-a-didip-didim-dow-hound
     You wonder bout the sweat upon my brow, formulatin nouns
     I'll get down, boogie brother rock on, right on, right on
     The brown rhyme, organically grown, I've shown, while
5   Sip-pida-didip-styles and proceed, to flow
     You know I'm flyer than G.I. So yo Joe…

     Datskat! I know you dig it when I kick it baby!
     Wadibi-dee-doo-bop-bop-bop-bop-bop
     Skiggy-dang, skiggy-dang, you knows we gonna rock
10   and don't stop…

Onomatopoeia: A Funny Word, Descriptive Sounds – Hip-Hop
Interpretation Guide

CA Language Arts Standards Covered:
9/10 LRA 3.7; L&S 1.1; W 2.2; W&O 1.3, 1.4; R 2.2 11/12 W&O 1.1, 1.2; W 2.2; R 2.0; LRA 3.4

Onomatopoeia: The use of a word whose sound imitates or suggests its meaning.

For example:
> Whoop, whoop, that's the sound of the police.
> Whoop, whoop, that's the sound of the beast.
> *(KRS-One)*

Identify the lines where the poet uses the technique of onomatopoeia in "Datskat".

- Line 1   Di-bi-dis-banks, hip-flip-a-didip-didim-dow-hound
- Line 5   Sip-pida-didip-styles
- Line 7   Datskat!
- Line 8   Wadibi-dee-doo-bop-bop-bop-bop-bop
- Line 9   Skiggy-dang, skiggy-dang

Explain what effect the use of onomatopoeia creates in the verse?

In the poem, the onomatopoeia is imitating the traditional jazz technique known as scat (or scatting). When jazz singers "scatted," they would imitate the sounds of other jazz instruments, such as horns, drums and bass. In this tradition, the poets infuse their words with these "scat" sounds. Using onomatopoeia here creates a jazzy effect in the verse giving them the same vividness that one would encounter in a jazz club while still maintaining the rap/lyrical flow for which Hip-Hop songs are known.

Onomatopoeia is added to the words "scat" (Line 5) and "styles (Line 7). What effect does this have?

Adding these sounds to the words "scat" and "styles" gives the words more texture. When the poet adds sounds to words they to carry more substance, more verbal and tonal weight.
In addition, they also bring aspects of language to a verse that is highly musical.
For example:

> "dat" (Line 7) is used like the word "that" but also blends the alliterative quality of ono-matopoeia and rhyme used throughout the verse.

Onomatopoeia: A Funny Word, Descriptive Sounds – Hip-Hop
Student Worksheet

Onomatopoeia: The use of a word whose sound imitates or suggests its meaning.

For example:
> Whoop, whoop, that's the sound of the police.
> Whoop, whoop, that's the sound of the beast.
> *(KRS-One)*

Identify the lines where the poet uses the technique of onomatopoeia in "Datskat".

_____

_____

_____

_____

_____

_____

Explain what effect the use of onomatopoeia creates in the verse?

_____

_____

_____

_____

_____

_____

Onomatopoeia is added to the words "scat" (Line 5) and "styles" (Line 7). What effect does this have?

_____

_____

_____

_____

_____

_____

Poetry Writing Exercise: Onomatopoeia

Learning Objective: Students will identify and utilize the poetic device of onomatopoeia.
Standards Addressed: 9/10 W&O 1.3, 1.4; LRA 3.7, 11/12 W&O 1.1, 1.2; W 1.5, 2.2
Materials needed: This worksheet.
Methodology: See below.

List three descriptive sounds that define the following items using a word whose sound imitates or suggests its meaning (i.e., onomatopoeia).

For example:

A bowl of Rice Crispies cereal   1. SNAP   2. CRACKLE   3. POP!

- The wind   1. _____   2. _____   3. _____
- Eating crackers   1. _____   2. _____   3. _____
- Fear   1. _____   2. _____   3. _____
- The beach   1. _____   2. _____   3. _____
- A puppy dog   1. _____   2. _____   3. _____

Create a POEM USING ONOMATOPOEIA:

A. Determine the subject of the poem.

B. Determine the effects you wish the sounds in the poem to create.

C. Choose an appropriate setting for the poem.

D. Use vivid language to complement your use of onomatopoeia.

For example:

The microphone

All eyes are on the microphone
Pft, Bumpt, Bumpt, Ptf
The beatboxer makes a pulse
come through the speakers like Whoosh!
Saliva drips from every ear
Soon we hear...
Budump! Boodoop! Budump! Boom Bap!!

Onomatopoeia Poem

_____

_____

_____

_____

_____

_____

_____

The Purpose of Pattern – Classic

If

by Rudyard Kipling

1   If you can keep your head when all about you
    Are losing theirs and blaming it on you,
    If you can trust yourself when all men doubt you
    But make allowance for their doubting too,
5   If you can wait and not be tired by waiting,
    Or being lied about, don't deal in lies,
    Or being hated, don't give way to hating,
    And yet don't look too good, nor talk too wise:

    If you can dream—and not make dreams your master,
10   If you can think—and not make thoughts your aim;
    If you can meet with Triumph and Disaster
    And treat those two impostors just the same;
    If you can bear to hear the truth you've spoken
    Twisted by knaves to make a trap for fools,
15   Or watch the things you gave your life to, broken,
    And stoop and build 'em up with worn-out tools:

    If you can make one heap of all your winnings
    And risk it all on one turn of pitch-and-toss,
    And lose, and start again at your beginnings
20   And never breath a word about your loss;
    If you can force your heart and nerve and sinew
    To serve your turn long after they are gone,
    And so hold on when there is nothing in you
    Except the Will which says to them: "Hold on!"

25   If you can talk with crowds and keep your virtue,
    Or walk with kings—nor lose the common touch,
    If neither foes nor loving friends can hurt you;
    If all men count with you, but none too much,
    If you can fill the unforgiving minute
30   With sixty seconds' worth of distance run,
    Yours is the Earth and everything that's in it,
    And—which is more—you'll be a Man, my son!

The Purpose of Pattern – Classic
Interpretation Guide

CA Language Arts Standards Covered:
9/10 LRA 3.4, 3.7, 3.9; L&S 1.1; W 2.2; W&O 1.3, 1.4; R 2.2 11/12 W&O 1.1, 1.2; R 2.0, 2.2, 2.4; LRA 3.3, 3.4.

Pattern: A combination of the organization of lines, rhyme schemes, stanzas, rhythm, and meter. (There are an innumerable variety of patterns in poetry.)

Poetic Theme: *Keep Your Head Up and Stay Strong*

What is the most obvious pattern in "If" and what is the effect it creates?

The repetition of the word "If" is the most obvious pattern in the poem. The effect the repetition of the word "If" creates is a sense that there is "strength" to be found in life for those who follow the advice of the poem. Those who respond to life's inevitable adversities in the manner advised by Kipling will discover almost a blueprint for living that will serve them well throughout their days. In other words, IF one can do this, then one will reap that.

Each stanza in "If" deals with a different aspect of life. What are the major themes Kipling addresses in each stanza?

In stanza one, the verse urges the reader not to deal in lies, hate or doubt. The main purpose of this stanza is to incite the reader to "trust yourself" (Line 3).

Stanza two revolves around the need to be levelheaded, sensible and calm as one marches through their days. "Triumph and Disaster" (Line 11) are not permanent states but rather simply false appearances (i.e., impostors) that will inevitably pass as time moves on. Kipling is saying that no one should be fooled into thinking that anything temporary is really eternal.

In stanza three (not unlike Eminem's Hip-Hop piece "Lose Yourself") the reader is asked if they can bounce back after risking everything and losing it all. IF you are unsuccessful and can "never breathe a word about your loss" (Line 20) and can maintain your will to "hold on" and keep fighting then the rewards at the end of the poem are available to be reaped.

The fourth stanza stresses the virtues of being down to earth, humble and not losing the "common touch" (Line 26). Furthermore, in Lines 29 & 30 the poet alludes to living each minute to the fullest, as time is a precious commodity, here for now—but then gone forever once it passes. Ultimately, IF the reader is able to accomplish these things, then they can rule their world (i.e., their "Earth") in a fulfilling, happy and satisfying manner.

If is considered by many to be an inspirational poem that encourages mankind to reach for their highest aspirations. Cite a sampling of lines that make references to mankind's highest aspirations.

- Line 3   "trust yourself"
- Line 9   "dream"
- Line 11   "meet Triumph and Disaster"
- Line 18   "risk it all"
- Line 24   " 'Hold on!' "
- Line 31   "Yours is the Earth and everything that's in it"

The Purpose of Pattern – Classic
Interpretation Guide *continued*

Although Kipling's poem "If" was written more than 100 years ago, do you think the advice he offers still holds true today? Why or why not?

Overall, the poem focuses on good virtues for living properly, honorably and intelligently, which are timeless themes that were true centuries ago and will still be true centuries from now. Being self-confident, loving and thoughtful is advice people still offer—and still heed—today.

In addition, a variety of other sensible advice exists, such as remaining patient, not falling victim to lies and hate, not becoming being too confident or cocky, and not giving up when all looks bleak. These ideas are also as relevant and important in our modern society as they were in Kipling's era. All in all, Kipling's wise words have very definite value to our contemporary society even though they were written more than 100 years ago.

The Purpose of Pattern – Classic
Student Worksheet

Pattern: A combination of the organization of lines, rhyme schemes, stanzas, rhythm, and meter. (There are an innumerable variety of patterns in poetry.)

What is the most obvious pattern in "If" and what is the effect it creates?

_____

_____

_____

_____

_____

_____

Each stanza in "If" deals with a different aspect of life. What are the major themes Kipling addresses in each stanza?

_____

_____

_____

_____

_____

_____

If is considered by many to be an inspirational poem that encourages mankind to reach for their highest aspirations. Cite a sampling of lines that make references to mankind's highest aspirations.

_____

_____

_____

_____

_____

Although Kipling's poem "If" was written more than 100 years ago, do you think the advice he offers still holds true today? Why or why not?

_____

_____

_____

_____

_____

The Purpose of Pattern – Hip-Hop

How Many

by Zion I

1   How many times have you watched the sun rise?
     How many times have you looked deep into your lovers eyes?
     How many times have we spit *phat* rhymes?
     How many times
5   How many times...

     How many times have you watched a full moon?
     How many times have you cried alone in your room?
     How many times have you felt the bass boom?
     How many times
10   How many times...

     How many times has a baby been born?
     How many times has lightning struck in a storm?
     How many times has your work been bought?
     How many times
15   How many times...

     How many times has the sky dropped rain?
     How many times has your heart felt pain?
     How many times mastered again and again?
     How many times
20   How many times...

The Purpose of Pattern – Hip-Hop
Interpretation Guide

CA Language Arts Standards Covered:
9/10 LRA 3.4, 3.7; L&S 1.1; W 2.2; W&O 1.3, 1.4; 11/12 W&O 1.1, 1.2; LRA 3.2, 3.3, 3.4 W 2.2; R 2.2, 2.4, 2.5

Pattern: A combination of the organization of lines, rhyme schemes, stanzas, rhythm, and meter. (There are an innumerable variety of patterns in poetry.)

Poetic Theme: We All Have Fears And Doubt

What is the most obvious pattern in How Many and what effect does it create?

The repetition of the phrase *How many times* is the most obvious pattern in the poem. (Another notable pattern is the rhyme scheme, including a series of end rhymes.) The use of repetition in the poem *How Many* creates an introspective mood by questioning the very essence of what we do as people while making us think about the significance and consequences of those actions.

What are some of the human emotions that the poet Zion I is exploring in his lyrics? What are some of the endeavors upon which he is reflecting?

On an emotional level, the poet is dealing with love ("looked deep into your lovers eyes," Line 2), anguish ("cried alone in your room," Line 7), and pain ("has your heart felt pain," Line 17). Some human endeavors that he explores are the act of rapping ("spit *phat* rhymes," Line 3), listening to music ("felt the bass boom," Line 8) and being rewarded for your efforts ("has your work been bought," Line 13).

In a more advanced sense, the speaker is shedding light on the circle of life starting with the birth (Line 11) and moving through human toil, love, anguish, and pain—all human experiences that occur within the natural cycle of life. In addition, by alluding to nature ("watched the sun rise," Line 1; "watched a full moon," Line 6; "lightning struck in a storm," Line 12; "the sky dropped rain," Line 16) the speaker almost implores the reader to be reflective on both the nature of the universe and our own places within it.

Identify the prominent How many's commonly shared by most people? How does the poet use these common experiences to connect with the reader?

The general feelings of love, pain (both physical and emotional), loneliness, work and awe of nature are all common human experiences. Though we experience them individually, we relate to one another as people by the commonality of the feelings these experiences create. The poet connects to the reader on an emotional level by citing these experiences creating empathy and emotional recognition in the reader. The poet also incites the reader to go out and experience a sunrise or a full moon or lightening or rainfall or listening to music and examine the profoundness of the simplicity of the event.

Does the poet think that one can ever experience any of these How many's enough times in their life? If not, explain why.

No, the poet seems to be implying that no matter how many times one has experienced any of these events, there is always a simple beauty to be found in experiencing them yet again. The question of "How Many" thus seems to be calling our attention to making sure that we, as people, recognize the important things—no matter how small or simple—that are of true value in this world.

The Purpose of Pattern – Hip-Hop
Student Worksheet

Pattern: A combination of the organization of lines, rhyme schemes, stanzas, rhythm, and meter. (There are an innumerable variety of patterns in poetry.)

What is the most obvious pattern in the lyrics of **How Many** *and what effect does it create for the reader?*

_____

_____

_____

_____

_____

_____

What are some of the human emotions that the poet Zion I is exploring in his lyrics? What are some of the endeavors upon which he is reflecting?

_____

_____

_____

_____

_____

Identify the prominent **How many**'s *that are commonly shared by most people? How does the poet use these common experiences to connect with the reader?*

_____

_____

_____

_____

_____

Does the poet think that one can ever experience any of these **How many**'s *enough times in their life? If not, explain why.*

_____

_____

_____

_____

_____

Poetry Writing Exercise: Pattern

Learning Objective: Students will identify and utilize the poetic device of pattern.
Standards Addressed: 9/10 W&O 1.3, 1.4; LRA 3.7, 11/12 R 2.2, 2.4; W&O 1.1, 1.2; W 2.2
Materials needed: This worksheet.
Methodology: See below.

Take two (or more) words and run them together to form one new, made-up word. Do this three times.

For example:

On + Sundays + I = OnSundaysI

1. _____ + _____ + _____ = _____
2. _____ + _____ + _____ = _____
3. _____ + _____ + _____ = _____

Now, choose your favorite word from your three new, made-up word creations to write an 8-line poem using your new, made-up word as the first word in every sentence.

For example:

Pattern Poem

OnSundaysI sleep late
OnSundaysI eat grapes
OnSundaysI pick up the phone and try to set up hot dates
OnSundaysI put on a hat
OnSundaysI tickle my cat
OnSundaysI jump in an online chat
OnSundaysI feel free
OnSundaysI am just ME!

Pattern Poem

_____ .
_____ .
_____ .
_____ .
_____ .
_____ .
_____ .
_____ .

Investigating Personification – Classic

Lodged
by Robert Frost

The rain to the wind said,
"You push and I'll pelt."
They so smote* the garden bed
That the flowers actually knelt,
And lay lodged*—though not dead.
I know how the flowers felt.

*Line 3: **Smote** = to strike or inflict a heavy blow upon.

*Line 5: **Lodge** = to beat down flat.

Investigating Personification – Classic
Interpretation Guide

CA Language Arts Standards Covered:
  9/10 LRA 3.7, 3.11; L&S 1.1; W 2.2; W&O 1.3, 1.4; R 1.1, 1.2, 2.2 11/12 W&O 1.1, 1.2; W 2.2; R 2.0, 2.5; LRA 3.4

Personification: A figure of speech in which an object or animal is given human feelings, thoughts, or attitudes.

For example:

My report card smiled, showing off straight A's.

Poetic Theme: The pain of life

Can the rain really talk to the wind? Can the wind really listen to the rain? Can the flowers really kneel?

In the way that people perform these acts, the answer is no. But if we *personify* the rain and the wind and the flowers and give them human qualities, the answer is yes.

What are some of the effects that the tool of personification brings to this poem?

- It makes the poem more interesting. If the rain is having a conversation with the wind about "beating up" the flowers, it makes us want to listen. We also want to see how the flowers react. Giving non-human objects human qualities adds spice and flavor to writing.
- It allows the readers to see things in a new and inventive manner.
  For example, in this poem we see the wind and the rain conspiring and collaborating as if they were rulers with unchecked power.

If the rain and wind and flowers were real people, how would one describe the event that is occurring?

Tyrannical, oppressive, bullying, ganging up.

If the flowers were real people, how do they feel after the wind and the rain "smote the garden bed"?

The flowers feel victimized and brutalized. They are in obvious pain. Though they are not dead (Line 5) they have undergone a very thorough thrashing which has left them much worse for the wear.

Speculate on why the speaker of the poem empathizes with the flowers?

Though there is no specific reason mentioned why the speaker of the poem empathizes with the flowers, it appears as if the speaker has undergone some sort of traumatic experience. Maybe it was external, such as being mugged and attacked in a dark alley. More probably though, this is a metaphor for some sort of life experience that has left the speaker feeling emotionally and spiritually ravaged.
  Some possible reasons are:
- The death of a loved one
- The breakup of a romance
- A personal failure or tragedy

Investigating Personification – Classic
Student Worksheet

Personification: A figure of speech in which an object or animal is given human feelings, thoughts, or attitudes.

For example:

My report card smiled, showing off straight A's.

Can the rain really talk to the wind? Can the wind really listen to the rain? Can the flowers really kneel?

_____ .
_____ .
_____ .
_____ .

What are some of the effects that the tool of personification brings to this poem?

_____ .
_____ .
_____ .
_____ .

If the rain and wind and flowers were real people, how would one describe the event that is occurring?

_____ .
_____ .
_____ .

If the flowers were real people, how do they feel after the wind and the rain "smote" the garden bed"?

_____ .
_____ .
_____ .
_____ .
_____ .

Speculate on why the speaker of the poem empathizes with the flowers?

_____ .
_____ .
_____ .
_____ .
_____ .

Investigating Personification – Classic & Contemporary

Mirror

by Sylvia Plath

1   I am silver and exact.
     I have no preconceptions.
     Whatever I see I swallow immediately.
     Just as it is, unmisted by love or dislike.
5   I am not cruel, only truthful—

I Am Music

by Common

1   You can feel me all over alive,
     I help culture survive, I opened the eyes of many
     Styles y'all wrote in the skies, with your lows and highs,
     open your mind to hear me
5   In the streets I beat cops and obsolete
     On every station it's hot you can't stop my heat
     I taught Jay and Dre how to rock the beat
     On what's going on today yo, I gots to speak
     I take the stand, yo you could feel me bam
10   Whether in Larry Graham or Steely Dan
     Live I be killing it man For how long I survived yo I'm realer than man
     Got a soft side but I'm still a man
     For me women cry and children dance,
     I'm trying to eat I could'a got a mil and ran
15   But like Sly for the fam still I stand
     I am music.

Investigating Personification – Classic & Contemporary
Interpretation Guide

CA Language Arts Standards Covered:
9/10 LRA 3.7, 3.11; L&S 1.1; W 2.2; W&O 1.3, 1.4; R 1.1, 1.2, 2.2 11/12 W&O 1.1, 1.2; W 2.2; R 2.0; LRA 3.4

Personification: A figure of speech in which an object or animal is given human feelings, thoughts, or attitudes.

For example:

My computer stared at me, deciding if it wanted to cooperate.

Poetic Theme: *Truth as a Matter of Perspective*

What are some of the "human" actions that the mirror takes in Plath's poem?

In the poem, the mirror is given the ability to speak in the first person, "I". The mirror can also see (Line 3), swallow (Line 3), and has the human ability to be both cruel and truthful (Line 5).

What kind of "human attitude" has the poet giving the mirror?

The mirror has an *attitude* of indifference, which comes across as cold and unfeeling. Since the mirror can only reflect the truth, it has no opinion or preconceptions other than that which is before it.

Plath is known for her sparse, stoic poems that leave the reader with shrill feelings of despair. Explain why this poem fits into that category?

This poem is typical of Plath because as humans, we don't just speak the truth, we take people's feelings into consideration. The mirror in the poem does not and as such, it comes off as an unfeeling, cold being that will tell us things we are scared to know about ourselves. Thus, if you truthfully engage with the mirror, you will be left with feelings of despair.

In "I Am Music," what are some of the "human" actions taken by music?

Music is personified in many ways. For example…
- Opens people's eyes (Line 2)
- Teaches other artists* how to ply their craft (Line 7)
- Takes a political stand (Line 9)

* This reference is relating to the famous DJ's/producers, Jam Master Jay and Dr. Dre.

What kind of "human attitude" has the poet given music?

Music is portrayed in a very positive light and has the attitude of being smooth, easy and "cool" in the poem. It also shows the flexibility to be compassionate, thoughtful, insightful, esoteric, inspirational, omnipresent and unstoppable.

The poet Common is known for his politically/spiritually conscious lyrics. Explain why his poem, "I Am Music" fits into that category?

I Am Music is typical of "Common" in the way that it pays homage to his musical ancestors (he makes reference to Jay, Dre, Steely Dan and Sly and the Family Stone), has a high political/spiritual value (Lines 8 & 9), and executes rhymes in a fresh, clever and creative manner.

Investigating Personification – Classic & Contemporary
Interpretation Guide

CA Language Arts Standards Covered:
9/10 LRA 3.2, 3.7, 3.11; L&S 1.1; W 2.2; W&O 1.3, 1.4; R 1.1, 1.2, 2.0, 2.2 11/12 W&O 1.1, 1.2; W 2.2; R 2.0; LRA 3.4

COMPARE AND CONTRAST: *Classic Poetry to Hip-Hop*

How are the poems of Plath and Common alike?

Answers will vary but...

- Both poets use the tool of personification.
- Both poets use the first person "I".
- Both poems have the theme of truthful reflection (but the mirror tells you the naked truth, while music appears to tell you what you want to hear).

How are the poems of Plath and Common different?

Answers will vary but...

- Plath is very specific about what a mirror is while Common shows how music can be many different things in many different ways.
- Plath is unsentimental about the mirror while Common is obviously very sentimental (in a positive manner) about Music.
- The mood of Plath's poem is scary and a bit daunting while the mood of Common's poem is warm and inviting.

Investigating Personification – Classic & Contemporary
Student Worksheet

Personification: A figure of speech in which an object or animal is given human feelings, thoughts, or attitudes.

For example: My computer stared at me, deciding if it wanted to cooperate.

What are some of the "human" actions that the mirror takes in Plath's poem?

_____

_____

What kind of "human attitude" has the poet given the mirror?

_____

_____

Plath is known for her sparse, stoic poems that leave the reader with shrill feelings of despair. Explain why this poem fits into that category?

_____

_____

_____

In "I Am Music," what are some of the "human" actions taken by music?

_____

_____

_____

What kind of "human attitude" has the poet given music?

_____

_____

_____

Common is known for his politically/spiritually conscious lyrics. Explain why his poem, "I Am Music" fits into that category?

_____

_____

_____

How are the poems of Plath and Common alike?

_____

_____

_____

How are the poems of Plath and Common different?

_____

_____

_____

Poetry Writing Exercise: Personification

Learning Objective: Students will identify and utilize the poetic device of personification.
Standards Addressed: 9/10 W&O 1.3, 1.4; LRA 3.7; R 1.1, 1.2, 11/12 W&O 1.1, 1.2; W 2.2
Materials needed: This worksheet.
Methodology: See below.

Personify 3 OBJECTS:

For example:

> The *report card smiled.*

1. _____ .
2. _____ .
3. _____ .

Personify 3 PLACES:

For example:

> My *house sang* the Blues.

1. _____ .
2. _____ .
3. _____ .

Write a PERSONIFICATION POEM where one of your chosen objects interacts with one of your chosen places.

For example:

Personification Poem

My report card smiled,
showing off straight A's.
My house no longer sang the Blues.
It's great to have happy grades,
and live in a neighborhood that is happy with you.

Personification Poem

_____

_____

_____

_____

_____

_____

_____

_____

Rhyme Examples – Classic
End, Internal, Half

In an END RHYME the rhyme occurs at the end of the verse lines. It is the most common rhyme form.

End Rhyme
Now my days are lonely,
And night-time drives me *wild,*
In my heart I'm crying,
I'm just Miss Blue'es *child!*
(Langston Hughes)

In an INTERNAL RHYME the rhyme occurs within a line of verse.

Internal Rhyme
The splendor *falls* on castle *walls*
And snowy summits old in story:
The long light *shakes* across the *lakes*
And the wild cataract leaps in glory.
(Alfred, Lord Tennyson)

In a HALF RHYME the rhyme is imperfect and approximate, not "dead on."

Half Rhyme
I was the slightest in the House—
I took the smallest *room—*
At night, my little Lamp, and Book—
And one *Geranium*
(Emily Dickinson)

Rhyme Scheme Identification Made Simple – Classic

Rhyme Scheme: the pattern of rhymes in a poem.

SIMPLE PATTERNS

Rhyme Scheme: (a, b, a, b)

> I laid me down upon a bank, (a)
> Where Love lay sleeping; (b)
> I heard among the rushes dank (a)
> Weeping, weeping. (b)
> *(William Blake)*

MORE COMPLEX PATTERNS

Rhyme Scheme: (a, b, a, b, c, c)

> I wandered lonely as a cloud (a)
> That floats on high o'er vales and hills, (b)
> When all at once I saw a crowd, (a)
> A host, of golden daffodils; (b)
> Beside the lake, beneath the trees, (c)
> Fluttering and dancing in the breeze. (c)
> *(William Wordsworth)*

COMPLEX RHYME PATTERNS

Rhyme Scheme: (a, b, a, a, b, c, c, d, a, d, a)

> In Xanadu did Kubla Khan (a)
> A stately pleasure-dome decree: (b)
> Where Alph, the sacred river, ran (a)
> Through caverns measureless to man (a)
> Down to a sunless sea. (b)
> So twice five miles of fertile ground (c)
> With walls and towers were girdled round: (c)
> And there were gardens bright with sinuous rills, (d)
> Where blossomed many an incense-bearing tree; (a)
> And here were forests ancient as the hills, (d)
> Enfolding sunny spots of greenery. (a)
> *(Samuel Taylor Coleridge)*

The Quality of Simile – Classic & Contemporary

Simile: A figure of speech that makes an explicit comparison between two unlike things, **using** the words **like** or **as.**

For example:

My shoes were like falcons, enabling me to fly across the basketball court.

Classic poets across the centuries have used similes to create a more in-depth and rich understanding of the feelings they seek to express.

For example:

What happens to a dream deferred?
Does it dry up
like a raisin in the sun?
(Langston Hughes)

My love is like a red, red rose,
That's newly sprung in June.
My love is like a melodie,
That's sweetly play'd in tune.
(Robert Burns)

I wandered lonely as a cloud
That floats high over the hills.
(William Wordsworth)

Hip-Hop artists also use similes as a tool to create a more in-depth and rich understanding of their feelings.

For example:

I love my baby's features
Like the creator loves all creatures.
(Mos Def)

I'm stuck to my mattress like crazy glue.
(Tupac Shakur)

Strong as cognac I got the knack to rhyme.
(LL Cool J)

When you liken one experience to another (using "like" or "as"), you create a simile.

For example:

- I am as gentle as a kitten.
- Jane dresses like a rainbow.
- Joe is as smart as Einstein.

Poetry Writing Exercise: Simile

Learning Objective: Students will identify and utilize the poetic device of simile.
Standards Addressed: 9/10 W&O 1.3, 1.4; LRA 3.7; R 1.1, 1.2; 11/12 W&O 1.1, 1.2; W 2.2; LRA 3.4
Materials needed: This worksheet.
Methodology: See below.

Create 3 SIMILES comparing sports to an object using "like" or "as."

For example: Football *is a like a war.*

1. _____ .
2. _____ .
3. _____ .

Create 3 SIMILES comparing a holiday to an object using using "like" or "as."

For example: Halloween *is like a candy store.*

1. _____ .
2. _____ .
3. _____ .

Create 3 METAPHORS comparing a person to an object using "like" or "as."

For example: My father *is like an encyclopedia.*

1. _____ .
2. _____ .
3. _____ .

Write a poem using at least 3 SIMILES comparing something important to you to how you feel about it.

For example:

Music Simile Poem

Hip-Hop is like a massage
   to my ears.
Hip-Hop is like the message
   of my tears.
Hip-Hop is as important
   as life,
Because Hip-Hop is art
   that gives insight.

_____

_____

_____

_____

_____

Sonnets Made Simple

Another Sonnet for Stephan

by Alvin Lester Sitomer

1   I see a little boy of four or five
    Whose face lights up whenever we would play
    Who made me feel it's great to be alive
    And wish that time would never tick away
5   I see a college youth who goes to Penn,
    Strong and handsome, smart in mind and dress,
    Enthusiastic, kind, who scores a "ten,"
    Possessing every trait that spells success.

    I see the man who came from both those boys
10 Creating business plans and paths to wealth
    With nonchalance, with skill and unique poise
    While fighting back attackers of his health.
    The boy, the youth, the man are each now gone,
    Except that in my heart they linger on.

Sonnets Made Simple
Interpretation Guide

A Special Section by Alvin Lester Sitomer

CA Language Arts Standards Covered:
9/10 LRA 3.7; L&S 1.1; W 2.2; W&O 1.3, 1.4; R 2.0, 2.2 11/12 W&O 1.1, 1.2; W 2.2; R 2.0, 2.2, 2.4; LRA 3.1, 3.4

Introduction:

Words are the building blocks of communication. They can be plain or fancy. For example, what young woman isn't more beautiful in a carefully tailored gown? What young man isn't more handsome in a tuxedo? So, it is with words.

The Sonnet is a form of well-dressed words.

But what specifically is a Sonnet?

A Sonnet is a poem which consists of the following building blocks:

1. A sonnet has 14 lines.

These lines are divided into 2 sections:
* The first section is called an octet (**8 lines**).
* The second section is called a sestet (**6 lines**).

For example:

1	I see a little boy of four or five	
	Whose face lights up whenever we would play	
	Who made me feel it's great to be alive	
	And wish that time would never tick away	**FIRST SECTION = OCTET**
5	I see a college youth who goes to Penn,	
	Strong and handsome, smart in mind and dress,	
	Enthusiastic, kind, who scores a "ten,"	
	Possessing every trait that spells success.	
	I see the man who came from both those boys	
10	Creating business plans and paths to wealth	
	With nonchalance, with skill and unique poise	**SECOND SECTION = SESTET**
	While fighting back attackers of his health.	
	The boy, the youth, the man are each now gone,	
	Except that in my heart they linger on.	

2. Each line in a sonnet has a special rhythm.

The rhythm is evidenced by an unstressed syllable followed by a stressed syllable.
For example:

> I **see** a **lit**tle **boy** of **four** or **five**
> Whose **face** lights **up** whenever **we** would play

(The stressed syllables are bold in the example above.)

FEEL THE RHYTHM. Notice that each unstressed syllable is immediately followed by a stressed syllable. (Reread the example: I **see** a **lit**tle **boy** of **four** or **five**.)

Sonnets Made Simple
Interpretation Guide

A Special Section by Alvin Lester Sitomer

3. Each line in a sonnet has a special length.
To measure length you must count the number of "iambs" in a sonnet.

An **iamb** is one unstressed syllable plus one stressed syllable.

For example:

I **see** a **lit**tle **boy** of **four** or **five**

These are the iambs: I **see**   a **lit**   tle **boy**   of **four**   or **five**

4. In a sonnet there are five iambs to each line. This is called a "pentameter."
Therefore...

Sonnets are written in iambic pentameter.

QUICK REVIEW

- A sonnet is 14 lines long.
- A sonnet is comprised of an octet (8 lines) plus a sestet (6 lines).
- Sonnets are written in iambic pentameter because each line has a special rhythm and a special length.
- An iamb equals 1 unstressed syllable plus one stressed syllable.
- There are 5 iambs in each line of a sonnet, thus it is called a "pentameter."

5. The rhyming scheme of the octet is "a" "b" "a" "b" "c" "d" "c" "d."

For example:

1   I see a little boy of four or five (a)
Whose face lights up whenever we would play (b)
Who made me feel it's great to be alive (a)
And wish that time would never tick away (b)   **FIRST SECTION = OCTET**
5   I see a college youth who goes to Penn, (c)
Strong and handsome, smart in mind and dress, (d)
Enthusiastic, kind, who scores a "ten," (c)
Possessing every trait that spells success. (d)

Sonnets Made Simple
Interpretation Guide

A Special Section by Alvin Lester Sitomer

6. *The sestet rhyming scheme is generally "e" "f" "e" "f" "e" "f".*

NOTE: The last two rhyming lines can be "g" "g." There are variations allowable in the scheme.
For example:

> I see the man who came from both those boys (e)
> 10   Creating business plans and paths to wealth (f)
> With nonchalance, with skill and unique poise (e)   **SECOND SECTION = SESTET**
> While fighting back attackers of his health. (f)
> The boy, the youth, the man are each now gone, (g)
> Except that in my heart they linger on. (g)

7. *The last 2 lines may contain a "heroic couplet."*
A heroic couplet is a two line thought which summarizes all of the poem's earlier lines.

For example:

> The boy, the youth, the man are each now gone, (g)
> Except that in my heart they linger on. (g)

NOTE: Please refer to the AP Exam section of this book for an accelerated analytical exercise relating to William Shakespeare's *Sonnet 18*.

Sonnets Made Simple
Student Worksheet

The Mechanics of a Sonnet

1. **How many lines are there in a sonnet?**

   _____

2. **There are two sections to a sonnet. What is the group of lines in the first section called?**

   _____

3. **How many lines are there in the first section (from question #2)?**

   _____

4. **What is the group of lines in the second section called?**

   _____

5. **How many lines are there in the second section (from question #4)?**

   _____

6. **What is an iamb?**

   _____

7. **In a sonnet, how many "iambs" are there to each line?**

   _____

8. **What is the official name of the line scheme in which sonnets are written?**

   _____

9. **Identify the rhyme scheme used in the first section of a sonnet?**

   _____

10. **Identify the rhyme scheme used in the second section of a sonnet?**

    _____

11. **The last two lines of a sonnet use a special rhyme scheme. What is this called?**

    _____

12. **What is the function of these last two lines?**

    _____

Sonnets Made Simple
Answer Key

The Mechanics of a Sonnet

1. **How many lines are there in a sonnet?**

   14 lines

2. **There are two sections to a sonnet. What is the group of lines in the first section called?**

   Octet

3. **How many lines are there in the first section (from question #2)?**

   8 lines

4. **What is the group of lines in the second section called?**

   Sestet

5. **How many lines are there in the second section (from question #4)?**

   Six

6. **What is an iamb?**

   An iamb is one unstressed syllable plus one stressed syllable.

7. **In a sonnet, how many "iambs" are there to each line?**

   There are 5 Iambs to each line.

8. **What is the official name of the line scheme in which sonnets are written?**

   Iambic Pentameter

9. **Identify the rhyme scheme used in the first section of a sonnet?**

   A - B - A - B - C - D - C - D

10. **Identify the rhyme scheme used in the second section of a sonnet?**

    E - F - E - F - G - G

11. **The last two lines of a sonnet use a special rhyme scheme. What is this called?**

    Heroic Couplet

12. **What is the function of these last two lines?**

    A two line thought which summarizes all of the poem's earlier lines.

Poetry Writing Exercise: Sonnet

Learning Objective: Students will identify and utilize the combination of tools necessary to write
                             their own technically correct sonnet.
Standards Addressed: 9/10 W&O 1.3, 1.4; LRA 3.7, 11/12 LRA 3.1; W&O 1.1, 1.2; W 1.5, 2.2
Materials needed: This worksheet.
Methodology: See below.

WRITE A SONNET

Rhyme Scheme

First Octet

Line 1 _____ (a)

Line 2 _____ (b)

Line 3 _____ (a)

Line 4 _____ (b)

Line 5 _____ (c)

Line 6 _____ (d)

Line 7 _____ (c)

Line 8 _____ (d)

Second Sestet

Line 9 _____ (e)

Line 10 _____ (f)

Line 11 _____ (e)

Line 12 _____ (f)

Heroic

Line 13 _____ (g)

Couplet

Line 14 _____ (g)

Tips to Remember

- A sonnet is **14 lines long.**
- A sonnet is comprised of an **octet (8 lines)** plus a **sestet (6 lines).**
- Sonnets are written in **iambic pentameter,** because each line has a special rhythm and a special length.
- An **iamb** equals one *unstressed* syllable plus one *stressed* syllable.
- There are five iambs in each line of a sonnet, thus it is called a "pentameter."
- The rhyming scheme of the octet is "a" "b" "a" "b" "c" "d" "c" "d."
- The rhyming scheme of the sestet is "e" "f" "e" "f" "g" "g."
- The last two lines form a heroic couplet.
- The **heroic couplet** is a two line thought which summarizes all of the poem's earlier lines.

Examining Symbolism – Classic

Sympathy

by Paul Laurence Dunbar

> I know what the caged bird feels, alas!
> When the sun is bright on the upland slopes;
> When the wind stirs soft through the springing grass,
> And the river flows like a stream of glass;
> 5   When the first bird sings and the first bud opes*,
> 6   And the faint perfume from its chalice* steals—
> I know what the caged bird feels!
>
> I know why the caged bird beats his wing
> Till its blood is red on the cruel bars;
> For he must fly back to his perch and cling
> 11   When he fain* would be on the bough a-swing;
> And a pain still throbs in the old, old scars
> And they pulse again with a keener sting—
> I know why he beats his wing!
>
> I know why the caged bird sings, ah me,
> When his wing is bruised and his bosom sore,—
> When he beats his bars and he would be free;
> It is not a carol of joy or glee,
> But a prayer that he sends from his heart's deep core,
> But a plea, that upward to Heaven he flings—
> I know why the caged bird sings!

Line 5: *opes* = opens

Line 6: *chalice* = a cup or goblet

Line 11: *fain* = happily, gladly

Examining Symbolism – Classic
Interpretation Guide

CA Language Arts Standards Covered:
9/10 LRA 3.4, 3.7; L&S 1.1; W 2.2; W&O 1.3, 1.4; R 1.1, 1.2, 2.0, 2.2 11/12 W&O 1.1, 1.2; W 2.2; R 2.0, 2.5 LRA 3.4

Symbols: A person, place, thing, or event that has meaning in itself and that also stands for something more than itself.

For example:

The eagle is a bird, but it is also the symbol for American freedom, liberty and justice.

Poetic Theme: The Human Spirit Needs to Be Free

What could the "caged bird" possibly be considered a symbol of?

Birds are very often representative of freedom. Therefore, a caged bird could be considered a symbol for something that is not free, that is restricted, confined or held back against its natural and instinctual will.

What are some elements outside of the bird's cage in the poem?
What could they be considered symbols for?

The sun on the slopes, the soft wind flowing throwing through the spring grass, and the flowing river (stanza one) are all creations of nature. Since they are unrestricted and allowed to uninhibitedly follow their own natural instincts, they too could be considered symbols of freedom—especially nature's freedom which has no real means of being restricted anyway (for how does one effectively imprison the sunshine or the wind?). In an extended sense, they can also be considered symbols for the human spirit, which can soar in an uninhibited manner when the soul is (or feels) free.

What are some prominent elements inside of the bird's cage?
What could they be considered symbols for?

Inside of the bird's cage we see "cruel bars" which have blood on them from the bird beating its wings in a desperate attempt to escape from the cage. The bird is obviously trying to escape from the cage, symbolic of the way in which the human spirit often tries to escape its own cage. This cage that imprisons the human spirit can be made of many things. Some of them include:

- oppression (i.e., tyranny by governments, bullying by tough kids at school)
- adversity (i.e., suffocating financial hardships, painful personal failures, setbacks)
- tragedy (i.e., the loss of a loved one, failing health)
- love (i.e., romantic heartbreak)

Why does the speaker claim to understand "what the caged bird feels" (stanza 1)?

The speaker seems to be claiming to understand what it feels like as a person to be trapped in a situation when one really desires to be free, unencumbered, and at liberty to choose one's own path.

Examining Symbolism – Classic
Interpretation Guide

Why does the speaker claim to understand "why he beats his wing" (stanza 2)?

The speaker seems to be claiming to understand what it feels like as a person to be fighting to escape being in a situation where one is trapped, imprisoned or held in a circumstance outside of one's own will to be there.

Why does the speaker claim to understand "Why the caged bird sings" (stanza 3)?

In stanza three we see that the singing is a prayer, not a song of joy or glee (Line 19). The bird sends this prayer from "his deep core" upward to heaven. The bird is basically praying with all its might for its freedom from the pain of the cage that oppresses it.

Furthermore, the speaker of the poem is obviously no stranger to the pains of life himself and therefore understands completely why the caged bird makes a beautiful plea to God above for freedom from imprisonment.

Why is the poem titled "Sympathy"?

The poem is titled "Sympathy" because the speaker:

1. Sympathizes, commiserates and shows compassion for the caged bird.

2. The speaker appears to understand the symbolism of "a caged bird" being able to witness the wonderful freedoms that exist outside of confinement without being able to enjoy them.

3. Most likely the speaker has prayed before, just like the caged bird is praying now. There is even a sense that the speaker knows that he will one day in the future pray again to the heavens above, much like the bird is doing now. It is as if it is the destiny of mankind to one day be in the same position as the caged bird, seeking relief through prayer from the only place that it can be granted: God.

Examining Symbolism – Classic
Student Worksheet

Symbols: A person, place, thing, or event that has meaning in itself and that also stands for something more than itself.

For example:

The eagle is a bird, but it is also the symbol for American freedom, liberty and justice.

What could the "caged bird" possibly be considered a symbol of?

_____

_____

_____

What are some elements outside of the bird's cage in the poem? What could they be considered symbols for?

_____

_____

_____

What are some prominent elements inside of the bird's cage? What could they be considered symbols for?

_____

_____

_____

Why does the speaker claim to understand "what the caged bird feels" (stanza 1)?

_____

_____

_____

Why does the speaker claim to understand "why he beats his wing" (stanza 2)?

_____

_____

_____

Why does the speaker claim to understand "Why the caged bird sings" (stanza 3)?

_____

_____

_____

Why is the poem titled "Sympathy"?

_____

_____

_____

Examining Symbolism – Hip-Hop

Three Strikes You In

by Ice Cube

1   One more strike and I'm through
Bottom of the ninth, swingin' for my life
I'm up at the plate, going for the gate
They got my moms seated in section eight...

5   Yeah, (It ain't right)
Playin' people like a game (It ain't right)
Human beings, puttin' em in a jar (It ain't right)
For double life, triple life (It ain't right)

    I gots to root for my homeboys
10 If they don't win it's a shame
Cuz it's one-two-three strikes you in
Twenty-five years of pain you know my name

Examining Symbolism – Hip-Hop
Interpretation Guide

CA Language Arts Standards Covered:
9/10 LRA 3.7, 3.11; L&S 1.1; R 1.1, 1.2; W 2.2; W&O 1.3, 1.4; 11/12 W&O 1.1, 1.2; W 2.2; LRA 3.2, 3.3, 3.4, 3.8

Symbols: A person, place, thing, or event that has meaning in itself and that also stands for something more than itself.

For example:

The eagle is a bird, but it is also the symbol for American freedom, liberty and justice.

Poetic Theme: The Human Spirit Needs To Be Free

Explain what baseball is being used as a symbol for in "Three Strikes You In."

Baseball is being used symbolically to describe the speaker's struggles in life (i.e., a minority, disenfranchised, American male's struggle). (*Ex:* "One more strike and I'm through," Line 1; "swingin' for my life," Line 2.)

The speaker is also using baseball as a symbolic metaphor to describe how he is being treated unfairly by society (*Ex:* "Playin' people like a game," Line 6; "swingin' for my life," Line 2). The game of baseball, as the speaker plays it, is therefore being used as a symbol for oppression and unjust struggle.

In "Three Strikes You In," what is the "In" to which Ice Cube refers?

The "In" that the speaker refers to is jail (i.e., being "in" prison. In Line 7 the speaker also uses a "jar" as a symbol of jail). The symbol of baseball, a game, is used to describe the penitentiary as a place where people are sent after three strikes. In baseball after three strikes, the player is sent to the dugout. In the state of California a prisoner, after three strikes is sent to jail with a minimum sentence of twenty-five years.

NOTE: this is the three strike rule in regards to mandatory jail sentencing in the state of California. (*Ex:* "Cuz it's one-two-three strikes you in/Twenty-five years of pain you know my name," Line 11 & 12.)

It is also notable to point out that the speaker's mother is seated in "section eight," (Line 4) which very clearly is a reference to Section 8 Housing—a symbol of very low-income, very economically disadvantaged housing in different parts of the country.

In the excerpts, baseball is a symbol of something that can be said to be hiding a deeper feeling about society. Describe what that feeling is.

In Ice Cube's lyrics, baseball is being used to describe the injustices that the speaker encounters in society. Baseball is, after all, America's "pastime," but the ugly side of American history—its pastime—is also riddled with slavery and oppression. The speaker is making a very clear parallel between the two.

"Shame" and "pain" are also two feelings the speaker could be said to be hiding. His reference to his "homeboys" (Line 9) is a symbolic identification with the common struggle of many minority males in the United States. The "twenty-five years of *pain*," is a reference to the mandatory sentencing of three-time offenders in the California penal system.

Examining Symbolism – Hip-Hop
Student Worksheet

Symbols: A person, place, thing, or event that has meaning in itself and that also stands for something more than itself.

For example:

The eagle is a bird, but it is also the symbol for American freedom, liberty and justice.

Explain what baseball is being used as a symbol for in "Three Strikes You In."

_____

_____

_____

_____

_____

In "Three Strikes You In," what is the "In" to which Ice Cube refers?

_____

_____

_____

_____

In the excerpts, baseball is a symbol of something that can be said to be hiding a deeper feeling about society. Describe what that feeling is.

_____

_____

_____

_____

_____

_____

_____

Poetry Writing Exercise: Symbolism

Learning Objective: Students will identify and utilize the poetic device of symbolism.
Standards Addressed: 9/10 W&O 1.3, 1.4; LRA 3.7, 3.11; R 1.1, 1.2 11/12 LAR 3.4; W&O 1.1, 1.2; W 2.2
Materials needed: This worksheet.
Methodology: See below.

A Symbol is a thing you can touch with your hands (i.e., it's tangible) but has some further meaning beyond itself.

For example:

> The Bald Eagle is more than just a bird,
> it is a symbol for the United States of America and its ideals.

I.   Identify what the following objects might be considered symbols for:

- A Red Rose   _____
- A Rolls Royce   _____
- A lion   _____
- A fork in the road _____
- The letter X   _____

II.   Create a list of 3 objects and explain what they are symbols of.

For example:

> My baggy pants are a symbol of my lifestyle.

1. My _____ is a symbol for_____ .
2. My _____ is a symbol for_____ .
3. My _____ is a symbol for_____ .

III. Write a four-line poem explaining the symbolism of an object from the list above.

For example:

My Baggy Pants

They're comfortable, reflect the style of my streets.
Sweatpants, jeans and khakis got beat.
I like it when my pants sag.
It doesn't really matter what name is on the tag.
It's a lifestyle.

Symbolism Poem

Title: _____

_____

_____

_____

_____

Understanding Tone – Classic

The Night has a Thousand Eyes

by Francis William Bourdillon

1   The night has a thousand eyes,
     And the day but one;
     Yet the light of the bright world dies
     With the dying sun.

5   The mind has a thousand eyes,
     And the heart but one:
     Yet the light of a whole life dies
     When love is done.

Understanding Tone – Classic
Interpretation Guide

CA Language Arts Standards:
9/10 LRA 3.7, 3.9, 3.11; L&S 1.1; W 2.2; W&O 1.3, 1.4; R 1.1, 1.2, 2.2 11/12 W&O 1.1, 1.2; W 2.2; R 2.0, 2.4, 2.5; LRA 3.3, 3.4

Tone: The attitude a writer takes toward the subject of a work, the characters, or the audience.

Poetic Theme: *Life is Nothing Without Love*

Does the night literally have eyes?

No. This is an example of figurative language in which the night (i.e., an object) is personified by being given human traits (i.e., eyes).

What is the most probable interpretation of the "thousand eyes" of the night that the speaker refers to?

The thousand eyes of the night could be stars in heaven looking down upon the events of earth.

What is the most probable interpretation of what the speaker is referring to in the line, "And the day but one" (Line 2)?

The sun is the one "eye" of the day.

What is the most probable interpretation of the "thousand eyes" of the mind that the speaker refers to?

The poet is probably referring to a person's thoughts.

When the speaker says "And the heart but one," (Line 6) what is the most probable interpretation that the speaker refers to here?

True love.

Does the sun ever really die? Does love ever really die?

No, not literally—figuratively.

If the sun or love does not ever really die, explain the tone of the speaker towards these objects.

The tone that the speaker takes towards both the sun and love is very positive as his point is that they are both essential to life. The speaker basically draws the comparison between how essential the sun is to the day and how essential love is to a life by pointing out that when one is gone, the "light" (of either the bright world or of a whole life) dies. (**NOTE:** It does not literally die, it metaphorically or symbolically dies—once again, we see a lot of figurative language).

What is the speaker's tone about how the deaths between the sun and love can be somewhat similar?

The speaker's tone is that the sun is the center of the day and that love is the center of life and if the "core" is taken out, there is nothing worthwhile left. Many parallel things are gone with the absence of these two things in our lives such as warmth, comfort, and nourishment. In addition, the void of these things is typically replaced with similar things such as coldness, loneliness and emptiness.

Understanding Tone – Classic
Student Worksheet

Tone: The attitude a writer takes toward the subject of a work, the characters, or the audience.

Poetic Theme: *Life is Nothing Without Love*

Does the night literally have eyes?

_____

What is the most probable interpretation of the "thousand eyes" of the night that the speaker refers to?

_____

_____

What is the most probable interpretation of what the speaker is referring to in the line "And the day but one" (Line 2)?

_____

What is the most probable interpretation of the "thousand eyes" of the mind that the speaker refers to?

_____

_____

When the speaker says "And the heart but one" (Line 6) what is the most probable interpretation that the speaker refers to here?

_____

_____

Does the sun ever really die? Does love ever really die?

_____

_____

If the sun or love does not ever really die, explain the tone of the speaker towards these objects.

_____

_____

_____

_____

What is the speaker's tone about how the deaths between the sun and love can be somewhat similar?

_____

_____

_____

_____

Understanding Tone – Hip-Hop

Paid In Full

by Rakim

1   Thinkin' of a master plan
     Cuz ain't nothing but sweat inside my hand
     So I dig into my pocket, all my money is spent
     So I dig deeper but still comin up with lint
5   So I start my mission- leave my residence
     Thinkin' how could I get some dead presidents
     I need money, I used to be a stick-up kid
     So I think of all the devious things I did
     I used to roll up, this is a hold up, ain't nothing funny
10 Stop smiling, be still, don't nothing move but the money
     But now I learned to earn cuz I'm righteous
     I feel great! So maybe I might just
     Search for a 9 to 5, if I strive
     Then maybe I'll stay alive…

Understanding Tone – Hip-Hop
Interpretation Guide

CA Language Arts Standards:
9/10 LRA 3.7, 3.9, 3.11; L&S 1.1; W 2.2; W&O 1.3, 1.4; R 1.1, 1.2, 2.2 11/12 W&O 1.1, 1.2;
W 2.2; R 2.4, 2.5; LRA 3.3, 3.4

Tone: The attitude a writer takes toward the subject of a work, the characters, or the audience.

Poetic Theme: Setting Goals

Why is the poet, "Thinking of a master plan" (Line 1)?

The poet is "thinking of a master plan" because he has no money. As he explicitly states, he has nothing but "sweat" in his hand (Line 2), and "lint" in his pocket (Line 4). He is "thinkin' of a master plan" because without one, his circumstances will not change.

What is the attitude (i.e., the tone) that the writer has towards money?

The poet's attitude is that he needs money in order to survive (just like all of us do) and fulfill his dreams. He claims to be on a "mission" (Line 5) to make "dead presidents" (Line 6). In Line 7, he even directly states, "I need money."

How did the poet make money in the past?

In the past, the poet claims to have been "devious" (Line 8) in his approach to making money. He was a "stick-up kid" (Line 7) who would rob people for their cash.

How does the poet now make his money?

While no specific details are given, the poet implies that he now makes his money legally, claiming to have "learned to earn" (Line 11). (**NOTE:** Being that Rakim is now a musical recording artist, this is probably the source of his revenue.)

What is the tone the poet takes towards how he used to make his money in the past and how does it differ from his tone about how he makes his money now?

The poet's tone towards his past endeavors sends mixed messages. On one hand, the poet seems to be bragging about his past criminal exploits. It's a "been there, done that" type of attitude he takes towards the life of crime. On the other hand, he readily acknowledges this is not the correct way to live one's life. We see this as the tone of the poem changes as the work progresses.

The poet literally seems to "grow up" in the course of this verse, recognizing that his lifestyle choice needed to change for the better. It wasn't until he infused his attitude with the aim of "righteousness" (Line 11), that he was able to "feel great" (Line 9). By proudly boasting that he now takes the more "righteous" path (Line 11) and he "feels great" as a result of it, we see how the shift has been made towards his beliefs about earning money.

This continues in Line 13 as the poet acknowledges the virtue of a "9-5" job and the rewards of striving for a noble means of employment. The ultimate benefit of which is that, "Then maybe I'll stay alive" (Line 14). This is another way of the poet saying that a life of crime puts one's life at risk.

Overall, as the poet's attitude matured he went from negative lifestyle choices to positive ones, reaping the benefits of the shift along the way.

Understanding Tone – Hip-Hop
Student Worksheet

Tone: The attitude a writer takes toward the subject of a work, the characters, or the audience.

Why is the poet, "Thinking of a master plan" (Line 1) ?

_____

_____

_____

What is the attitude (i.e., the tone) that the writer has towards money?

_____

_____

_____

How did the poet make money in the past?

_____

_____

_____

How does the poet now make his money?

_____

_____

_____

What is the tone the poet takes towards how he used to make his money in the past and how does it differ from his tone about how he makes his money now?

_____

_____

_____

_____

_____

_____

_____

_____

_____

Poetry Writing Exercise: Tone

Learning Objective: Students will identify and utilize the poetic device of tone.
Standards Addressed: 9/10 W&O 1.3, 1.4; LRA 3.7, 11/12 R 3.3; W&O 1.1, 1.2; W 1.5, 2.2
Materials needed: This worksheet.
Methodology: See below.

Make a list of three objects.

For example: Sushi, Rodents, Campfires

1. _____   2. _____   3. _____

Pick one of the objects and write a four-line poem expressing a POSITIVE TONE (i.e., a positive feeling) towards that object.

For example: Sushi

Fresh from the ocean
Resting on rice
Raw fish in my belly
Ooh, it's so nice!

Your Object: _____

_____
_____
_____
_____

Pick the same object and write a four-line poem expressing a NEGATIVE TONE (i.e., a negative feeling) towards that object.

For example: Sushi

Uncooked and raw?
Just reeled in and cut
How can you eat that?
Barf, Barf, Yuck!

Your Object: _____

_____
_____
_____
_____

Pick the same object and write a four-line poem expressing a NEUTRAL TONE (i.e., absent of feeling) towards that object.

For example: Sushi

A portion of rice
A piece of fish
A touch of seaweed
Served on a dish

Your Object: _____

_____
_____
_____
_____

Additional

Poetic

Resources

Making Sense of Poetry
Using Reading Strategies

JABBERWOCKY

by Lewis Carroll

'Twas brillig, and the slithy toves
Did gyre and gimble in the wabe:
All mimsy were the borogoves,
And the mome raths outgrabe.
5   "Beware the Jabberwock, my son!
The jaws that bite, the claws that catch!
Beware the Jubjub bird, and shun
The frumious Bandersnatch!"
He took his vorpal sword in hand:
10   Long time the manxome foe he sought—
So rested he by the Tumtum tree.
And stood awhile in thought.
And, as in uffish thought he stood,
The Jabberwock, with eyes of flame,
15   Came whiffling through the tulgey wood,
And burbled as it came!
One, two! One, two! And through and through
The vorpal blade went snicker-snack!
He left it dead, and with its head
20   He went galumphing back.
"And, hast thou slain the Jabberwock?
Come to my arms, my beamish boy!
O frabjous day! Callooh! Callay!"
He chortled in his joy.
25   'Twas brillig, and the slithy toves
Did gyre and gimble in the wabe:
All mimsy were the borogoves,
And the mome raths outgrabe.

Making Sense of Poetry Using Reading Strategies
Interpretation Guide

CA Language Arts Standards Covered:
  9/10 LRA 3.7, 3.9; L&S 1.1; W 2.2; W&O 1.3, 1.4; R 2.2, 2.4, 2.5; 11/12 LRA 3.3, 3.4 W&O 1.1, 1.2; W 2.2; R 2.0

"Jabberwocky" is a poem from Lewis Carroll's book, "Through the Looking-Glass and What Alice Found There."

Reading Strategies:

Context Clues:	Using words surrounding unknown words to determine their meaning.
Inferring:	Giving a logical guess based on the facts or evidence presented using prior knowledge to help "read between the lines."
Drawing Conclusions:	Using written cues to figure out something that is not directly stated.
Rereading:	Giving the reader more than one chance to make sense of challenging text.
Summarizing:	Guiding the reader to organize and restate info, usually in written form.

As a poem, "Jabberwocky" uses a lot of nonsense words, but one can still understand the basic story. The reading strategies above are the primary means for this.

Explain what a Jabberwock is? (They will need to Reread the poem.)

Make sure to have students cite specific references from the poem to support their explanation. **(SKILLS:** Drawing Conclusions, Inferring, Context Clues, Rereading.)

The Jabberwock is some sort of monster with "jaws that bite" (Line 5) and "claws that catch" (Line 5) and "eyes of flame" (Line 14).

The Jabberwock "burbled" (Line 16). What does it means to "burble? How did you arrive at this definition?
(SKILLS: Rereading, Drawing Conclusions, Inferring, Context Clues.)

To burble, while making no literal sense, seems to mean something bad and potentially danger-ous. (This is revealed through *context clues, inferences and conclusions drawn* from the events taking place in the poem.) We know there is a boy fighting an apparently fierce Jabberwock, so if the Jabberwock burbles as it approaches the boy, it seems to mean danger and peril await the hero of the story.

Briefly summarize the story being told by Lewis Carroll in the poem.
(SKILLS: Summarizing, Rereading, Drawing Conclusions, Inferring, Context Clues.)

The story is essentially about a brave boy who slays the fierce Jabberwock. This is revealed to us because…
- We know the boy is brave because he fights a scary monster with a sword (like heroes in the tales of old).
- We know the monster is scary and dangerous (see the explanation of a Jabberwock above).
- We also know the boy wins the fight ("He left it dead," Line 19).

Making Sense of Poetry Using Reading Strategies
Interpretation Guide *continued*

What does "Callooh! Callay!" mean?
(SKILLS: Rereading, Drawing Conclusions, Inferring, Context Clues.)

The exclamations of "Callooh! Callay!" are cries of joy. We deduce this because:

- The words are preceded by "O frabjous day!" which seems very close in meaning to the phrase "O fabulous day!"
- Joy at the news that the dreaded Jabberwock has been slain is an apt response.
- The lines have been described as having been "chortled in joy" (Line 24) which lend further proof that they are positive in nature.

NOTE: *Part of being a good reader is following intuition.*

SIDE NOTE: Here's what Alice (from the book) had to say about the poem…

"It seems very pretty," she said when she had finished it, *"but it's rather hard to understand!"*
(You see she didn't like to confess even to herself, that she couldn't make it out at all.)
"Somehow it seems to fill my head with ideas—only I don't exactly know what they are! However, somebody killed something: that's clear, at any rate—"

Making Sense of Poetry Using Reading Strategies
Student Worksheet

As a poem, "Jabberwocky" uses a lot of nonsense words, but one can still understand the basic story. Use the following reading strategies:

Context Clues:	Using words surrounding unknown words to determine their meaning.
Inferring:	Giving a logical guess based on the facts or evidence presented using prior knowledge to help "read between the lines."
Drawing Conclusions:	Using written cues to figure out something that is not directly stated.
Rereading:	Giving the reader more than one chance to make sense of challenging text.
Summarizing:	Guiding the reader to organize and restate info, usually in written form.

Remember, part of being a good reader is *following your intuition.*

Explain what a Jabberwock is? (Reread the poem.) Cite specific references from the poem to support your explanation. (**SKILLS:** Drawing Conclusions, Inferring, Context Clues, Rereading.)

_____

_____

_____

_____

The Jabberwock "burbled" (Line 16). What does it means to "burble?
How did you arrive at this definition?
(**SKILLS:** Rereading, Drawing Conclusions, Inferring, Context Clues.)

_____

_____

_____

_____

Briefly summarize the story being told by Lewis Carroll in the poem.
(**SKILLS:** Summarizing, Rereading, Drawing Conclusions, Inferring, Context Clues.)

_____

_____

_____

_____

What does "Callooh! Callay!" mean?
(**SKILLS:** Rereading, Drawing Conclusions, Inferring, Context Clues.)

_____

_____

_____

_____

Author's Choice – Classic

The Tide Rises, The Tide Falls

by Henry Wadsworth Longfellow

1   The tide rises, the tide falls,
    The twilight darkens, the curlew calls;
    Along the sea-sands damp and brown
    The traveller hastens toward the town,
5   And the tide rises, the tide falls.

    Darkness settles on roofs and walls,
    But the sea, the sea in the darkness calls;
    The little waves, with their soft, white hands,
    Efface the footprints in the sands,
10 And the tide rises, the tide falls.

    The morning breaks; the steeds in their stalls
    Stamp and neigh, as the hostler calls;
    The day returns, but nevermore
    Returns the traveller to the shore,
15 And the tide rises, the tide falls.

Author's Choice – Classic
Interpretation Guide

CA Language Arts Standards Covered:
9/10 LRA 3.7, 3.11; L&S 1.1; W 2.2; W&O 1.3, 1.4; R 1.1, 1.2, 2.2 11/12 W&O 1.1, 1.2;
W 2.2; R 2.02.2, 2.4, 2.5; LRA 3.4

Poetic Theme: Life goes on

Identify the rhyme scheme used by Longfellow in "The Tide Rises, the Tide Falls."

- Longfellow uses the pattern of A,A,B,B,A in the first stanza.
- Longfellow uses the pattern of A,A,C,C,A in the second stanza.
- Longfellow uses the pattern of A,A,D,D,A in the third stanza.

How does the poet's choice of rhyme scheme seem to match the theme of the poem?

The rhyme scheme is a fairly simple one but yet there is a pattern and a purpose. The reason the rhyme scheme matches so well with the theme of the poem is because essentially, life operates in a very similar manner: basically, an argument can be made that life is a very simple process which has a pattern and a purpose (though we may, as people, not always necessarily know what it is).

Literal Interpretation vs. Figurative Interpretation

In lines 8 & 9, the poet writes, "The little waves, with their soft, white hands / Efface the footprints in the sands." These lines can be interpreted either literally or figuratively. Please interpret them both ways.

Literal Interpretation: The traveller has left visible footprints from walking on the beach. As the tide comes in, the small waves wash over the footprints and fresh sand, like a blank canvas, is left along the shoreline when the tide goes back out.

Figurative Interpretation: The traveller's footprints are a symbolic representation of all the efforts we make as people. Some examples are the work we do at our jobs, the bank deposits for which we wait in line, the homework assignments we worry about when we put them off until the last minute, etc. ... But time, like the waves on the beach, eventually wipes away all of our color televisions, birthday presents and moments of frustration. In the end, despite the ups and downs and twists and turns, none of it will really matter, as life will go on with or without us (i.e., "The tide rises, the tide falls").

In lines 13 & 14 the poet writes, "The day returns, but nevermore/ Returns the traveller to the shore." These lines can be interpreted either literally or figuratively. Please interpret them both ways.

Literal Interpretation: The traveller who entered the town (Line 4) has spent the night but, being a traveller, has moved on with the new day never to return again. Such is the nature of travellers as they move on from place to place.

Figurative Interpretation: The traveller is a symbolic representation of all of us as individuals on this planet with our individual lives to live. We move throughout our existences, going from here to there until the day comes when we "are called" (Line 11) and nevermore return to earth. But life goes on (i.e., "The tide rises, the tide falls").

Author's Choice – Classic
Student Worksheet

Identify the rhyme scheme used by Longfellow in "The Tide Rises, the Tide Falls."

_____

_____

_____

How does the poet's choice of rhyme scheme seem to match the theme of the poem?

_____

_____

_____

_____

Literal Intepretation vs. Figurative Intepretation

In Lines 8 & 9, the poet writes, "The little waves, with their soft, white hands / Efface the footprints in the sands." These lines can be interpreted either literally or figuratively. Please interpret them both ways.

Literal Interpretation: _____

_____

_____

_____

_____

Figurative Interpretation: _____

_____

_____

_____

_____

In lines 13 & 14 the poet writes, "The day returns, but never more / Returns the traveller to the shore." These lines can be interpreted either literally or figuratively. Please interpret them both ways.

Literal Interpretation: _____

_____

_____

_____

_____

Figurative Interpretation: _____

_____

_____

_____

_____

Author's Choice – Hip-Hop

Fight the Power

by Public Enemy

Got to give us what we want
Got to give us what we need
Our freedom of speech is freedom or death
We got to fight the powers that be...

5   We got to pump the stuff to make us tough from the heart
It's a start, a work of art
To revolutionize make a change nothin's strange
People, people we are the same
No we're not the same
10 Cause we don't know the game
What we need is awareness, we can't get careless
You say what is this?
My beloved let's get down to business...

Author's Choice – Hip-Hop
Interpretation Guide

CA Language Arts Standards Covered:
9/10 LRA 3.3, 3.4, 3.7, 3.9; L&S 1.1; W 2.2; W&O 1.3, 1.4; R 3.0; 11/12 LRA 3.8; W&O 1.1, 1.2; W 2.2; R 3.0

Public Enemy's "Fight the Power" is a shining example of Hip-Hop poetry with political consciousness.

What does the title mean, "Fight the Power"?

The title, "Fight the Power" is a political call to action to change the existing power structure in society. This power structure exists in all facets of society including electoral politics, socioeconomics, education, law and social services.

Locate lines from the verse that give the poem a political nature and explain why.

- Line 3: The author addresses exercising freedom of speech, a reference to our constitutional rights to do so.
- Line 4: The author cites "the powers that be." This is usually the government, but can be applied to any part of society where unfairness/injustice/oppression exists.
- Line 7: "To revolutionize make a change," is a call to take political action.

In Line 2, what is it that "we need"?

In Line 11, the poet explains that, "What we need is awareness."

Explain the meaning of Line 3, "Our freedom of speech is freedom or death"?

Essentially, the poet is saying that his freedom of speech is what determines his freedom. If he doesn't use his voice, it could mean death.

Explain what the poet means in Lines 8 & 9?

The poet is addressing the notion that all people are created equal in Line 8. This is one of the basic tenets of our Constitution. However, he follows up that line with, "No we're not the same" (Line 9). This line challenges the notion of equality and highlights the inequity in our society—that people are not equal.

The poet further explains that a part of this iniquity is due to people NOT knowing the "game" (Line 10). Inequities in education and economic opportunity over lines of race and class perpetuate this cycle of empowerment and disenfranchisement. Thus, people do not have the same opportunities, and "awareness" (Line 11).

Political speakers use different techniques to "rally" the masses.
Identify the lines where the poet could be said to be "rallying his audience" through verse.

- Lines 1 & 2: Chuck D is demanding equality from "the powers that be" and outlines what they have to do. "Got to give us what we want/ Got to give us what we need."
- Line 4: The poet incites his audience to "fight" for their rights.
- Line 10: The poet urges the audience to "get down to business" after letting them know that they are his "Beloved."

Author's Choice – Hip-Hop
Student Worksheet

Public Enemy's Fight the Power is a shining example of Hip-Hop poetry with political consciousness.

What does the title mean, "Fight the Power"?

_____
_____
_____
_____

Locate lines from the verse that give the poem a political nature and explain why.

_____
_____
_____
_____

In Line 2, what is it that "we need"?

_____
_____
_____
_____

Explain the meaning of Line 3, "Our freedom of speech is freedom or death"?

_____
_____
_____
_____

Explain what the poet means in Lines 8 & 9?

_____
_____
_____
_____

Political speakers use different techniques to "rally" the masses.
Identify the lines where the poet could be said to be "rallying his audience" through verse.

_____
_____
_____
_____

Authors Choice – Hip-Hop

Otha Fish

by The Pharcyde

1   It took a second to register up in my branium
    My dome, my head, my skull, my cranium
    My eyes have had enough, it was time to do some talkin
    I had to creep through the hound-dogs that were stalkin
5   This slimmy caught me peepin, this means she wasn't sleepin
    On who I was, so she crept in like a hawk
    In a minute's time, we adjourned to the floor
    Ooh! I hit a high note cause of the way that she was walkin
    We got into the groove, I didn't bust no, uh, hip-hop moves
10 I just kept it nice and smooth…

Authors Choice – Hip-Hop
Interpretation Guide

CA Language Arts Standards Covered:
Standards: 9/10 LRA 3.7; L&S 1.1; W 2.2; W&O 1.3, 1.4; 11/12 W&O 1.1, 1.2; W 2.2;

Identify some of the literary elements utilized in this verse.

- The first, most obvious, literary device that the author uses is rhyme scheme. There are internal rhymes (Line 5, "sleepin/peepin"), end rhymes (Lines 1 & 2, "branium/cranium") and half rhymes (Lines 9 & 10, "moves/smooth"). Elaborate rhyme schemes are common in Hip-Hop.
- In Line 6, the author uses the simile, "crept in like a hawk."
- In Lines 8 & 9, the author uses onomatopoeia with the words "Ooh" and "uh."

Why does the writer "invent" the word brainium in Line 1?

The writer is seeking to use especially vivid language and description in order to make this event abundantly clear. Stretching the rules of proper English brings a particularly rich and memorable description to this verse.

Describe the events taking place in this verse.

In this verse the author begins by looking at and admiring a girl who he obviously finds attractive. He then decides he should talk to her, after stepping through her other admirers ("hound-dogs that were stalkin," Line 4).

After a quick minute, he escorts her to the dance "floor" and they get into their "groove" (Line 9) where he then plays it cool.

Authors Choice – Hip-Hop
Student Worksheet

Identify some of the literary elements utilized in this verse.

_____

_____

_____

_____

_____

Why does the writer "invent" the word brainium in Line 1?

_____

_____

_____

_____

_____

Describe the events taking place in this verse.

_____

_____

_____

_____

Write a short poem describing the events from a time when you thought about approaching someone you "admired from a distance."

_____

_____

_____

_____

_____

_____

_____

_____

_____

_____

_____

_____

Authors Choice – Hip-Hop

Lose Yourself

by Eminem

His palms are sweaty, knees weak, arms are heavy
There's vomit on his sweater already, mom's spaghetti
He's nervous, but on the surface he looks calm and ready
To drop bombs, but he keeps on forgetting
5   What he wrote down, the whole crowd goes so loud
He opens his mouth both the words won't come out
He's choking, how? Everybody's joking now
The clock's run out, time's up, over —BLAOW! …
He's so mad, but he won't
10   Give up that easy, nope, he won't have it
He knows, whole back's to these ropes
It don't matter, he's dope
He knows that, but he's broke
He's so sad that he knows
15   When he goes back to this mobile home, that's when it's
Back to the lab again, yo…
He better go capture this moment and hope it don't pass him

You better lose yourself in the music, the moment
You own it, you better never let it go
20   You only get one shot, do not miss your chance to blow
This opportunity comes once in a lifetime.

Authors Choice – Hip-Hop
Interpretation Guide

CA Language Arts Standards Covered:
   Standards: 9/10 LRA 3.7; L&S 1.1; W 2.2; W&O 1.3, 1.4; 11/12 W&O 1.1, 1.2; W 2.2;

*In Lines 1-3, explain where the poet uses the literary device of **internal rhyme** in the verse.*

- Line 1   Rhyme Scheme A/B/A (sweaty, arms, heavy)
- Line 2   Rhyme Scheme A/C/A/ (already, mom's, spaghetti)
- Line 3   Rhyme Scheme D/D/C/A (nervous, surface, calm, ready)

*Identify where the poet uses the literary device of **onomatopoeia** in his verse.*

- Line 8   The author uses onomatopoeia with "BLAOW!"

*Identify where the poet uses the literary device of **allusion** in his verse.*

- Line 4   "to drop bombs" (meaning he is ready to "unleash" his rap poetry)
- Line 8   "The clock's run out" (a reference to Hip-Hop "battles" being performed under a timed format. In addition, this is a play on words as "time" is metaphorically running out on the poet achieving his dreams.)
- Line 11   "back's to these ropes"—(meaning his back is up against the ropes of socioeconomic depravity and abject failure is staring him right in the face).

*Identify areas in the verse where the poet uses particularly rich detail and vivid language to create strong **imagery** in the work.*

- Line 1   "palms are sweaty, knees weak, arms are heavy"
            —we can literally see the nervousness.
- Line 2   mom's spaghetti has been vomited on his sweater. Very vivid language.
- Line 6   "opens his mouth but the words won't come out"—a classic example of a performer "freezing" on stage.
- Line 15   he lives in a "mobile home."

The **meaning** of this verse is about overcoming adversity. What are some of the insights that the author gives into his adversity, and how did he overcome them?

In the first five lines, the author is clearly nervous and unable to perform. One of the ways he tries to overcome this problem is by maintaining a "calm" disposition (Line 3). When the speaker finally does "choke" (Line 7), he shows that he "won't give up that easy, nope, he won't have it" (Lines 10 & 11).

In Lines 11-15, the speaker goes between being self-aware of his shortcomings and his promise. He knows that he has his back against the "ropes" (Line 11), but also that he is "dope" (Line 12). ("Dope" is a slang term for being good, skilled, or talented.) In Lines 11 & 15, the speaker knows that he is poor and living in a "mobile home," but also that it is his "lab" (Line 16) where he will go to "capture" his dreams.

Finally, Lines 18-21 (the chorus of the song) carry the meaning of *losing yourself* in order to overcome adversity and reach personal victory. It is the "moral" to this verse.

Authors Choice – Hip-Hop
Student Worksheet

In Lines 1-3, explain where the poet uses the literary device of **internal rhyme** *in the verse.*

_____

_____

_____

Identify where the poet uses the literary device of **onomatopoeia** *in his verse.*

_____

_____

Identify where the poet uses the literary device of **allusion** *in his verse.*

_____

_____

_____

_____

_____

_____

_____

Identify areas in the verse where the poet uses particularly rich detail and vivid language to create strong **imagery** *in the work.*

_____

_____

_____

_____

_____

_____

The **meaning** *of this verse is about overcoming adversity. What are some of the insights that the author gives into his adversity, and how did he overcome them?*

_____

_____

_____

_____

_____

_____

Poetry Recital Exercise
Memorizing and Performing a Classic Poem

Learning Objective:	To gain a deeper understanding of a particular poem's meaning via an in-depth study and oral presentation of the work.
Standards Addressed:	9/10 L&S 1.7, 1.9, 1.11, 2.4; 11/12 L&S 1.4, 1.7, 2.5
Materials needed:	A Classic Poem (student's choice)
Methodology:	See below.

Memorize and Perform a Poem

HOW TO PREPARE

1. *Read through your poem silently.*

2. *Think about the speaker of the poem (and characters).*

3. *Ask yourself:*
   a. What is this speaker feeling?
   b. What meaning is this speaker trying to get across?
   c. What do you think this speaker sounds like?

For more advanced presentations ask...

   d. What do you think this speaker looks like?
   e. How do you think this speaker moves (slowly, quickly, proudly...)?

4. *Think about how you can best portray this speaker through:*
   a. Voice
   b. Body
   c. Facial expression
   d. Props

5. *PRACTICE!! The only way to memorize a poem is to practice memorizing the poem. There are no shortcuts.*

TEACHING TIP #1: *Students may want to underline key words that need emphasizing or write instructions on the poem itself such as "be loud" or "slam fist" or "SHOUT!", etc.*

(**NOTE:** Allowing students to bring their poems to the front of the room with them is at the teacher's discretion.)

TEACHING TIP #2: *Allow the students some time to practice aloud with their peers. It is much easier to recite a poem aloud with dramatic flair after having done so in front of people a few times prior. Having only practiced the poem in one's head or alone may not prove to be enough practice for an effective class presentation of the poem.*

Poetry Recital Exercise
Memorizing and Performing a Classic Poem

One of the Best Pick-Up Poems Ever Written

MEMORIZE THIS.

Share it with that "special someone."
Get results.

Love's Philosophy
by Percy Bysshe Shelley

The fountains mingle with the river
And the rivers with the ocean,
The winds of heaven mix for ever
With a sweet emotion;
Nothing in the world is single,
All things by a law divine
In one another's being mingle—
Why not I with thine?

See the mountain's kiss high heaven
And the waves clasp one another;
No sister-flower would be forgiven
If it disdain'd its brother:
And the sunlight clasps the earth,
And the moonbeams kiss the sea—
What are all these kissings worth,
If thou kiss not me?

Poetry Recital Exercise
Oral Interpretation

Learning Objective:	To have students learn the importance of varying the pitch, rate and volume of their voices and recognize how this can impact the interpretation of a poem.
Standards Addressed:	9/10 L&S 1.1, 1.7, 1.9, 1.11, 2.4; R 2.0; 11/12 LRA 3.3; R 2.0; L&S 1.4, 1.7, 2.5
Materials needed:	A Classic Poem (open to choice)
Methodology:	See below.

1. *Divide students up into groups of three.*

2. *Have each group select a "classic" poem.*
   (Classic works better than Hip-Hop for this activity.)

SAMPLE POEM:

A Child's AMAZE

by Walt Whitman
SILENT and amazed, even when a little boy,
I remember I heard the preacher every Sunday put God in his
statements,
As contending against some being or influence.

3. *Have students take turns reading the poem emphasizing one word over the others.*

For example:

   The first student can read the Whitman poem emphasizing "I" and the second student can read the poem emphasizing "God" and "preacher," but diminish the importance of "I" in the poem. *(The effect that the poem has will be drastically different.)*

4. *Discuss how the meaning of the poem changes as different words are emphasized.*

5. *As the students listen to other poems, instruct them to recognize how word emphasis plays a large role in the ultimate meaning of the work.*

Some poems that lend themselves well to this activity are:

   We Real Cool by Gwendolyn Brooks

   Do Not Go Gently Into That Goodnight by Dylan Thomas

   Jabberwocky by Lewis Carroll

   If by Rudyard Kipling

   Ain't I a Woman? by Sojourner Truth

   Lodged by Robert Frost

   The Tide Rises, The Tide Falls by Alfred Lord Tennyson

   Harlem: A Dream Deferred by Langston Hughes

Poetry Recital Exercise
Assuming an Identity

Learning Objective: To have students learn the importance of varying the pitch, rate and volume of their voices and recognize how this can impact the interpretation of a poem.
Standards Addressed: 9/10 L&S 1.7, 1.9, 1.11, 2.4; 11/12 L&S 1.4, 1.7, 2.5
Materials needed: A Classic Poem (open to choice)
Methodology: See below.

Poems sometimes require the use of a different voice, but a great many students are reluctant to "embarrass" themselves by reciting a poem with a dramatic flair.

TO GET THEM TO "STEP OUT OF THEIR SHELL" ...

1. Have students assume the character of another person reading the poem.

This allows students to shelter themselves a bit behind the mask of "acting" and brings a lot of fun to a classroom recital.
For example:

2. Have students read a poem (teacher or student choice) in the voice of...

- Their own mother.
- A Police Officer.
- A Rapper.
- A Shakespearean Actor.
- A thug.

3. Allow the class to be creative in the selection of their voices.

4. For Group activities...

Have the class read the same poem in different voices and discuss how the meaning of the poem changes as different words, accents and mannerisms are employed.

TEACHING TIP #1: *Encourage your students to have fun with this exercise. Have them vary their volume, pitch and rate greatly. Remind them to over-exaggerate and to be as dramatic as possible.*

TEACHING TIP #2: *Allow the students some time to practice aloud with their peers. It is much easier to recite a poem aloud with dramatic flair after having done so in front of people a few times prior. Having only practiced the poem in one's head or alone may not prove to be enough practice for an effective class presentation of the poem.*

Poetry Recital Exercise
Performing Team Poems

Learning Objective: To gain a deeper understanding of a poem's meaning via an in-depth study and oral presentation of the work.
Standards Addressed: 9/10 LRA 3.7; L&S 1.1, 1.7, 1.9, 1.11, 2.4; 11/12 L&S 1.4, 1.7, 2.5
Materials needed: A Poem (student's choice)
Methodology: See below.

Team poem performances are fun, exciting, and bring lots of fresh energy to the material on the page.

HAVE STUDENTS:

1. *Pair off with another classmate (or two).*

2. *Select a poem to perform. (Teacher approval is recommended.)*

3. *Divide up which person will be reciting which lines.*

4. *Practice! Groups need to create a "flow" between them.*

5. *Incorporate non-verbal elements into the presentation.*

   For example:

   If one partner is speaking about a robot, the partner not speaking could be moving like a robot in the background. Be creative.

6. *Incorporate props, costumes or music (if you wish).*

Poetry is creativity so BE CREATIVE!

7. *Remember, that the element of surprise can be a strong component.*

   For example:

   Have a fellow classmate become a contributor by shouting out one line of the group poem from their chair in the back of the room. This will take everyone by surprise and add a bit of excitement to the reading.

8. *Some lines may be spoken in unison to provide more depth, texture and punch!*

Poetry Recital Exercise
How to Host a Poetry Slam
A poetry slam is a contest in which poets perform original work before an audience.

- From this audience five, randomly selected judges, will score the poets
- The scale will range from 1-10 (Olympic style, preferably using decimal points to avoid ties).
- Seek to select "impartial" people to do the judging.

YOU WILL NEED:

- Poets
- Judges
- An MC
- A location

- Refreshments (well, they add a nice touch)
- Prizes for the winners.
  (Just a suggestion—and money is NOT needed.
  A day without homework, extra-credit… be creative.)

HISTORY OF SLAMS: Poetry Slam was started in 1986 by a construction worker and poet, Marc Smith, at a Chicago jazz club called The Green Mill. It was a way to make poetry reading exciting and to get audiences more involved in the process. In a slam, audience members are encouraged to hoot and holler for the poems they admire. Judges are encouraged to stay consistent with their scores, and not be influenced by the audience.

1. **To start a slam it is best to have 10 or more poets who are willing to have their poems judged.**

   They should understand that the criteria on which they will be judged is based on their poem and their performance. In adult slams almost all of the poets have their poems memorized. For student slams, leeway is granted and pupils can bring their written work to the stage.

2. **The person organizing the slam selects 5 judges from the audience.**

   These judges are to understand that they are to judge the poets on a 1–10 scale, using decimal points. They will base their scores on both the content and performance of the poem.
   (**NOTE:** It is also important that judges try to stay consistent with their scores. Many judges have the tendency to inflate their scores as the competition goes on *[a phenomenon known in the slam world as Score Creep]*.)

3. **Provide the judges with blank sheets of paper and markers to write their scores.**

4. **The order of poet performance is randomly picked (out of a hat type of thing).**

5. **The poets will be introduced (by the MC) and allowed to perform their poem.**

6. **After the poet has finished, the audience should be encouraged to cheer for the poet.**

   A long-standing slam motto is that the poet is not the points, it is the poetry. (i.e., encourage contestants to write quality works for which they will be rewarded. This is not performance art —it is about the words).

7. **The 5 judges will hold up their scores.**

8. **The host will read the score aloud, drop the highest and lowest score, then add up the total of the three remaining scores.**

9. **The poet with the most points at the end of the slam wins!**

Poetry Recital Exercise
Acrostics

Learning Objective:	To have students gain flexibility in their approach to the use of language.
Standards Addressed:	9/10 W&O 1.3, 1.4; LRA 3.7, 11/12 W&O 1.1, 1.2; W 2.2
Materials needed:	This Worksheet
Methodology:	See below.

In ACROSTIC POEMS,
the first letters of each line are aligned vertically to form a word.
The word often is the subject of the poem.

I. Pick 3 objects that inspire excitement in you.

For example: Hip-Hop

    1. _____

    2. _____

    3. _____

II. Choose one of the three objects about which you wish to write a poem.

III. Print the first letter of each word vertically (i.e., down) the page.

IV. Write a poem about the object that you selected using the first letter of your chosen object as the start to each new line.

For example:

        Happiness in music
        Inspires my song
        Pulses like my heart
        Hot lyrics make me strong
        On in the morning and when I go to bed
        Praise for the music that plays in my head

Acrostic Poem

_____ _____

_____ _____

_____ _____

_____ _____

_____ _____

_____ _____

_____ _____

_____ _____

_____ _____

_____ _____

_____ _____

Activities
Create an Autobiographical Poem

Fill in the blanks to lay the foundation for writing an original autobiographical poem.

Welcome to My Life by _____

Welcome to my life. It is more fascinating than _____.

From the second I wake I hear _____.

It reminds me that, "_____."

"Through the haze and the daze that lead to lonely ways," I always _____

_____.

This makes me _____.

When I am _____ , I get _____.

_____ like _____, like _____,

Like _____.

This is my life not yours, you don't understand my _____.

Your definition of what _____ means is different than mine

because in my world _____

_____

_____.

Welcome to my life. For fun I like to _____.

It makes me happier than _____.

In the electric heaven I call _____.

I always make sure that _____ will guide me on the right path.

In my life, my favorite person is _____.

S/he is as _____ as a _____.

S/he makes me feel _____

when I hear the _____ sound of his/her _____ voice.

It takes me into the _____ heavens and never makes my life seem _____

_____ because _____

is my _____.

Activities
Create an Autobiographical Poem continued

Welcome to my life _____.

In my world all you see is _____, _____, _____,

and _____ for miles.

In my world, the style is _____. People wear everything from_____

_____ to _____. The styles are _____.

As for me, I'm like _____.

My personality is like _____.

My main purpose in life is to _____.

It is as _____ as _____.

When I achieve my goals I feel _____

_____

_____.

I want to share my world with_____.

Because in my life I feel_____

_____

_____

_____.

If there were three words to sum up my life, they'd be: _____.

Welcome.

_____
ASSIGNMENT:

Using any aspect of the material you just created, write an original, autobiographical poem based on your own life.

Activities
Similes and Metaphors

My _____ (street) is like _____.

The neighborhood reminds me of _____.

After being at school all day long my house feels like _____.

It smells as _____ as _____.

My bedroom is my _____.

It is where my _____(s) begin.

I close my _____ eyes, and _____ is what I see.

My dreams are _____ like_____.

My mind is a _____.

My heartbeat sounds like _____.

Car horns _____ outside my window like _____.

Children play _____ and run like _____

until it is time for dinner. The food smells like _____.

My nose becomes _____.

My belly is _____.

I am as satisfied as a _____.

When dinner is finished it is time for _____ homework.

It is as _____ as _____

and when I am finished I feel like a _____.

This is when I like to _____

because when I _____ I am as _____

as _____.

Activities
Create a Poetry Journal

A Cumulative Project

Learning Objective: To gain a deeper understanding of poetry's meaning, complexity, elements and components via an in-depth study and compilation of original work.
Standards Addressed: 9/10 W&O 1.3, 1.4, 1.5; W 1.8; 1LRA 3.7, 11/12 W&O 1.1, 1.2; W 2.2.
Materials needed: A folder (or binder) for each student.
Time needed: Two weeks (minimum) — A semester (possible).
Methodology: See below.

Creating poetry journals is a great way to have all members of the class work towards the publication of an extensive written project that incorporates original writing, research, and critical thinking.

INFORM YOUR CLASS THAT...

I. Each student will compile his or her own poetry journal.

II. Each student will contribute 3 pages relating to each specific poetic element assigned for this journal.

- One page will be a classic poem
- One page will be a Hip-Hop poem
- One page will be an original poem

For example:

In a poetry journal's section on ALLUSION...
  1. one page would be dedicated to a classic poet who used allusion (i.e., Sojourner Truth's *Ain't I a Woman?*)
  2. one page would be dedicated to a Hip-Hop poet who used allusion (i.e., Talib Kweli's *For Women*)
  3. one page would be dedicated to a student's original poem using allusion

III. Each poetry journal will have:

- An illustrated cover
- A title page
- A table of contents
- The student' name prominently displayed
- 3 pages from each poetic element covered in class (teacher discretion)
- Illustrations
- An autobiographical poem
- Their favorite Classic Poem
- Their favorite Hip-Hop Poem

PLEASE SEE FOLLOWING PAGE

(**NOTE:** The choice of elements and the amount of elements has been left to the teacher's discretion.)
One teacher may do a two-week project covering only five poetic elements.
Another teacher may do a semester-long project covering 17 poetic elements.
We have left it up to you.

Activities
Poetry Journal Grading Rubric

Name _____

POETRY PAGE EVALUATION

1. _____   Name displayed on each page. (1-5)

2. _____   Illustrated Journal Cover (1-5)

3. _____   Typed Title Page (1-5)

4. _____   Typed Table of Contents (1-5)

5. _____   Classic Poem Authors properly noted (1-5)

6. _____   Hip-Hop Poem Authors properly noted (1-5)

7. _____   Original Poems properly written (1-5)

8. _____   Illustrations for original poems (1-5)

9. _____   Autobiographical Poem (1-5)

10. _____   Favorite Classic Poem and why (1-5)

11. _____   Favorite Hip-Hop Poem and why (1-5)

12. _____   Pages submitted on time (1-5)

13. _____   Spelling and Grammar (1-5)

14. _____   Organization (1-5)

15. _____   Neatness (1-5)

_____   **TOTAL POINTS**

Activities
Hip-Hop Poetry Word Search

```
s  k  j  c  q  r  r  k  y  o  o  y  v  j  w  z  e  t  s  b  m  g  w
n  h  m  o  u  e  k  x  p  p  j  z  z  e  v  n  a  w  c  l  o  m  m
i  v  a  n  o  s  n  i  k  c  i  d  i  z  y  l  c  b  o  a  s  m  x
u  r  d  k  n  o  t  o  r  i  o  u  s  b  i  g  q  o  i  k  d  i  w
v  m  q  z  e  p  s  e  s  n  n  a  s  b  j  y  n  y  m  e  e  k  h
c  j  t  a  l  s  b  n  r  r  m  c  k  p  s  e  h  f  a  m  f  s  a
h  w  n  a  u  u  p  k  l  o  k  w  e  a  h  l  e  s  y  b  o  d  x
d  t  t  c  s  k  e  h  e  e  d  h  y  e  l  o  i  z  b  g  n  g
o  h  u  e  t  i  y  t  a  l  c  r  e  u  i  e  t  l  k  e  a  t  s
t  n  c  r  s  x  e  n  i  r  t  b  e  j  t  h  n  v  p  q  j  s  l
i  i  o  e  t  z  n  n  j  k  e  u  j  b  d  s  p  e  m  z  s  v  t
p  w  m  s  n  h  z  r  n  e  q  x  d  s  k  t  y  r  h  r  m  y  y
f  r  b  x  y  d  m  t  o  o  g  z  x  k  c  c  n  s  g  v  u  v  j
p  r  h  c  m  n  q  p  h  i  n  u  j  v  u  g  f  t  i  c  x  v  z
z  y  o  v  w  w  n  a  w  m  h  f  a  r  h  v  t  e  o  f  b  l  h
v  d  z  s  u  d  z  e  c  l  g  n  c  a  c  h  m  i  n  h  g  t  i
x  g  e  c  t  x  v  c  t  l  s  s  p  z  i  m  t  n  e  w  y  j  p
a  k  o  p  k  h  c  a  p  u  t  i  b  y  h  d  i  x  n  q  j  i  u
h  u  g  h  e  s  d  i  o  a  b  n  u  s  d  b  x  c  y  a  d  g  j
n  x  n  w  h  x  v  g  i  f  s  o  o  a  z  n  d  h  e  b  j  n  v
d  e  i  f  v  x  s  k  p  v  k  i  f  w  i  o  f  r  q  q  c  v  x
o  e  e  j  c  h  z  r  k  x  t  z  t  c  i  j  r  g  i  e  x  v  c
m  e  n  i  m  e  q  r  j  c  z  u  u  p  h  o  q  d  v  w  i  j  j
```

Find the poets (Classic and Hip-Hop) in the jumble above:

Blake	Keats	Shakespeare
ChuckD	KRSOne	Shelley
Common	MosDef	Talib Kweli
Dickinson	Nas	Tennyson
Eminem	NotoriousBIG	Thomas
Frost	Plath	Truth
Hughes	Poe	Tupac
IceCube	RunDMC	ZionI

Activities
Hip-Hop Poetry Word Scramble

Unscramble the words below.

(**HINT:** *They are all elements of poetry.*)

1. odom . . . . _____

2. onte . . . . _____

3. revs eerfe . . . . _____

4. uihka . . . . _____

5. eopryeblh . . . . _____

6. riymeag . . . . _____

7. ryino . . . . _____

8. mnengai . . . . _____

9. hmpeaort . . . . _____

10. onalertaltii . . . . _____

11. otnepooomaia . . . . . . _____

12. anptter . . . . _____

13. eoiitfinpnsaroc . . . . . _____

14. eryhm . . . . _____

15. tymrhh . . . . _____

16. lsemii . . . . _____

17. sonetn . . . . _____

18. mineti ambteecpar . _____

19. osimmbysl . . . . _____

20. oulnalsi . . . . _____

21. oyprte . . . . _____

22. hpo hpi . . . . _____

23. ipehtpa . . . . _____

Activities
Hip-Hop Poetry Word Scramble

Answer Key

1.	odom	....	**mood**
2.	onte	....	**tone**
3.	revs eerfe	....	**free verse**
4.	uihka	....	**haiku**
5.	eopryeblh	....	**hyperbole**
6.	riymeag	....	**imagery**
7.	ryino	....	**irony**
8.	mnengai	....	**meaning**
9.	hmpeaort	....	**metaphor**
10.	onalertaltii	....	**alliteration**
11.	otnepooomaia	....	**onomatopoeia**
12.	anptter	....	**pattern**
13.	eoiitfinpnsaroc	....	**personification**
14.	eryhm	....	**rhyme**
15.	tymrhh	....	**rhythm**
16.	lsemii	....	**simile**
17.	sonetn	....	**sonnet**
18.	mineti ambteecpar	.....	**iambic pentameter**
19.	osimmbysl	....	**symbolism**
20.	oulnalsi	....	**allusion**
21.	oyprte	....	**poetry**
22.	hpo hpi	....	**Hip-Hop**
23.	ipehtpa	....	**epitaph**

AP Exam Success

Achieving High Scores on the Advanced Placement English Literature and Composition Exam (POETRY).

INITIAL STRATEGY

I. *Read the poem through one time. Try to...*

- **Identify the tone of the poem.**
  - Is the speaker elated, despondent, ambivalent, remorseful, etc.?
    (**NOTE:** If this is too tough to decipher, just try to get a feel for whether or not the speaker is positive, negative or neutral.)

- **Identify the general meaning of the poem.**
  - Is this a poem celebrating the glory of life, the vagueness of death, the blush of a fair maiden's cheek, etc.? In very simple terms, try to paraphrase the poem's basic meaning.

- **Identify who the speaker of the poem probably is.**
  - Is the speaker a male, female, child, adult, religious fanatic, anarchist, coffee cup or a kitten? Know who is speaking?

II. *Read the poem through a second time... more slowly.*

- **Read the poem again line by line.**
  - Try to grasp the words, concepts, ideas and references.
  - Look for imagery, symbols and figurative language that give objects in the poem a meaning beyond the object itself.

- **Underline, mark up the page, take notes.**
  - Turn the poem into a worksheet whereby you are breaking down all of your thoughts and ideas on the page. Paraphrase, underline, do what you feel you must, but DO NOT JUST COUNT ON YOUR MEMORY—WRITE ON THE TEST!

- **Reread lines three and four times if necessary.**
  - This doesn't mean spend all day on a particular line, but it does mean that sometimes it takes a while to grasp the gist of a line. It's a natural part of the process.

- **Do not be afraid of words / ideas you do not understand!**
  - One can do quite well without grasping 100% of the poem.
    Focus on what you do know, not what you do not.

MOVE ON TO THE QUESTIONS...

AP Exam Success
Multiple Choice Strategy

I. *Read the question thoroughly.*

- **Understand what is being asked of you.**
  - A great many students encounter problems because they do not take the time to completely and clearly comprehend the question being asked and thus they fall into "answer traps."

II. *Know your poetical terms excellently well BEFORE taking the test.*

- **Every poetic element in this book must be familiar to you!**
  The test covers everything. At the very least, you must know…
- Allusion, alliteration, epitaph, figurative language, hyperbole, iamb, imagery, irony, meaning, metaphor, mood, motif, onomatopoeia, pattern, personification, rhyme scheme, simile, sonnet, symbolism, theme, tone.

III. *Eliminate wrong answer choices.*

- **Use the process of elimination.**
  - There are four wrong answers and only one right one for every multiple choice question. That means 80% of the answers are wrong. Weed them out and get rid of them as soon as possible.

IV. *When given a line reference, make sure to read the lines before and after the specified line in order to build context for understanding.*

- **Do not just read the referenced line. Read around the lines.**

V. *Expect to face a wide spectrum of questions.*

- **The AP exam will ask technical, interpretative, historically contextutal, thematic and comparison/contrast questions** (and more).
  - You will need to make inferences. The answers are very rarely "hard and fast" or "obvious."

VI. *Guessing*

- **If you can eliminate two or more answers, guess.**
  - If not, skip the question and return if time allows.

VII. *Understand time management.*

- **The AP exam is a timed test — so do not spend too much time on any one question.**
  - If, after employing all of the prior strategies, the question simply stupefies you, SKIP IT AND MOVE ON.

AP Exam Success
Essay Question Strategy

I. *Read the question carefully.*

- **Understand what is being asked of you.**
  - Address ALL aspects of the question in your response.

II. *Organize your essay.*

- **To score well, AP essays *must* contain the following structural elements.**
  (NOTE: A 5 paragraph structure is highly recommended.)
  - *Section 1 — The Introduction*
    - Addresses the Main Idea of the essay
    - Includes a Thesis Statement
  - *Section 2 — Body Part I*
    - Contains a specific point which is a subtopic of the main idea.
    - Provides supporting information addressing this subtopic using an example, detail, fact, logical reason or incident.
    - Directly references specific aspects of the poem.
  - *Section 3 — Body Part II*
    - Contains a specific (but different) second point which is a subtopic of the main idea.
    - Provides supporting information addressing this subtopic using an example, detail, fact, logical reason or incident.
    - Directly references specific aspects of the poem.
  - *Section 4 — Body Part III*
    - Contains a specific (but different) third point which is a subtopic of the main idea.
    - Provides supporting information addressing this subtopic using an example, detail, fact, logical reason or incident.
    - Directly references specific aspects of the poem.
  - *Section 5 — Conclusion*
    - Summarizes the essay.
    - Addresses the thesis.
    - Does NOT introduce any new information.

III. *Use vivid language.*

- **Strong writing uses strong language. Be descriptive.**

IV. *Make sure to identify, address and write about literary terms.*

- **Scorers want to see your knowledge of such things as figurative language, hyperbole, meter, etc.**

V. *Proofread for proper spelling, grammar and punctuation.*

- **Take the time to insure a high degreee of quality.**
  - Try to have been neat (or at least legible).
  - Don't try to be perfect—none of us are. Seek to be excellent!

AP Exam Success
Sample Essay Prompt

TIME ALLOTTED: 40 MINUTES

Read the following poem carefully, then write a well-organized essay in which you discuss both the technical and interpretive aspects of the work. Be sure to consider such literary elements as structure, imagery, figurative language, meaning and point of view.

Sonnet 18

by William Shakespeare

Shall I compare thee to a summer's day?
Thou art more lovely and more temperate:
Rough winds do shake the darling buds of May,
And summer's lease hath all too short a date:
5   Sometime too hot the eye of heaven shines,
And often is his gold complexion dimm'd;
And every fair from fair sometime declines,
By chance, or nature's changing course, untrimm'd;
But thy eternal summer shall not fade,
10   Nor lose possession of that fair thou owest;
Nor shall Death brag thou wander'st in his shade,
When in eternal lines to time thou growest;
        So long as men can breathe, or eyes can see,
        So long lives this, and this gives life to thee.

AP Exam Success
Sample Essay Answer Rubric

PLEASE NOTE:

This page will only address the contents of the essay.
Refer to the page "AP Exam Success — Essay Question Strategy" for a complete guideline about how the essay should be organized and structured.

In order to score well on the AP Sample Essay prompt a student would have needed to address the following:

I. *The Technical Aspects of Shakespeare's "Sonnet 18"*

- It is written in 14 lines of iambic pentameter
  - An iamb is a stressed then an unstressed syllable
  - Pentameter means there are five iambs to a line
- There are two main sections to the sonnet
  - An octet (the first 8 lines)
    - The rhyme scheme for the octet is A – B – A – B – C – D – C – D
  - A sestet (the last 6 lines)
    - The rhyme scheme for the sestet is E – F – E – F – G – G
      - The G – G rhymes scheme that ends to sonnet is called a heroic couplet.
      - The purpose of a heroic couplet is to summarize the thoughts of the poem.

II. *The Interpretive Aspects of "Sonnet 18"*

- The poem begins with a question that appears almost unfair but in a clever turn, our expectations are turned upside down.
  - What person could compare to a shining example of nature's finest beauty (i.e., A Summer's Day)?
  - In the second line, we see that it is the Summer's Day that does not fair well in the comparison.
  - Thus we see that this is going to be a love poem.
    - Thus we infer that the speaker is a man in love.
    - Thus we infer that the audience for the poem is a young maiden with whom the speaker is smitten.
- In Line 3, Shakespeare begins using the poetic device of imagery.
  - He evokes a clear picture of the "rough winds" shaking gentle flower buds to point out the faults of a Summer's Day compared to the beauty of the maiden his is addressing in the poem.
  - In Line four, he discusses how summer does not stick around forever, thus pointing out more flaws in the season.
- In Line 5 the poetic tool of personification is introduced as the poet gives an object human qualities.
  - Line 5, the "eye of heaven" (i.e., the sun).
  - Line 6, "complexion dimm'd" is used as if it were a human feature.

AP Exam Success
Sample Essay Answer Rubric *continued*

- Essentially, the first section of the poem (i.e., the octet) is dedicated to citing the flaws of a summer's day, and as the second section of the poem begins (i.e., the sestet), Shakespeare moves from finding fault with nature to distinguishing praise for the maiden being addressed in the poem.
    - In Line 9 the poet explains how the maiden's eternal summer will always be around.
        - This is an example of figurative language. She will not literally always be in a state of eternal summer. She will only figuratively be in a state of eternal summer.

- The meaning of Death not being able to brag about how "thou wandere'st in his shade" is worth noting for a few reasons:
    - Death is capitalized in Line 11 as if it were a person (thus more figurative language and personification is utilized).
    - The shade of Death is an allusion to a place with there is no light.
        - Literally, this could be six feet under the earth.
        - Figuratively, this could be the dark realms of hell.
    - The meaning of this line can also be read as a nod to immortality because Death claims us all—except for the maiden being addressed in the poem. How? This is answered by the heroic couplet.

- The heroic couplet that ends this poems accomplishes a few notable points:
    - It uses a variety of poetic devices.
        - A pattern is established as the two words "So Long" begin each line.
        - The poetic tool of alliteration is used in Line 12 "long lives."
        - There is an internal, half rhyme used in Line 11 "breathe" "see."
    - It summarizes the poem's main point that the maiden compares more favorably to a summer's day.
        - This is done by explaining how a summer's day eventually ends but, through the writing and future reading of this poem, the maiden's best virtues will live on and on and be exhorted until this sonnet no longer is read by mankind.
        - And five hundred years later, we are still reading it.
        - This shows how Shakespeare understood a degree of where his historical position in the study of literature might ultimately be.

The AP Essay Analysis covers the following CA Language Arts Standards:
    Grades 9/10: W&O 1.1, 1.2, 1.3, 1.4; W 1.0, 1.1, 1.2, 1.4, 1.6, 1.9, 2.2, 2.3, 2.4 LRA 3.7, 3.9, 3.11, R 1.1, 1.2, 2.0;
    Grades 11/12: LRA 3.1, 3.2, 3.3; W&O 1.1, 1.2; R 2.0 2.2, 2.4; W 1.3, 1.5, 1.9, 2.2

Gifted and Talented Education
G.A.TE. Differentiation

Unique Projects for Gifted and Talented Students

1. *Research the life of a classic poet and a Hip-Hop poet.* **Create a learning center** *comparing the fashion, music, and entertainment of the your chosen classic poet to the life of your Hip-Hop poet.*

   - Hypothesize how each of them would fair if they were to exchange historical places with one another.
     - a. How would their poetry be different?
     - b. How would their poetry be the same?
   - Recite a work from each of your chosen poets but use the language of their counterpart. For example:
     - a. Rewrite the classic poet's poem using Hip-Hop vocabulary.
     - b. Rewrite the Hip-Hop poet's poem using classical vocabulary.

2. *Many poets are accused of being slanderous, crude, and obscene (both classic and Hip-Hop).* **Stage a mock trial** *whereby the classroom puts a classic poet and a Hip-Hop poet on trial and debates the subject of artistic expression and free speech vs. the moral harm and implications of letting just anyone say anything they want.*

   - Keep in mind two adages:
     - a. That just because one does not like the speech of another man, it does not mean that this man's speech should not be free.
     - b. Free speech does not mean that one can shout "Fire!" in a crowded movie theater due to the detriment and harm it may cause to others.
   - The trial should be based on research:
     - a. into the potential harm caused by the language.
     - b. the rights of the artists.
     - c. the history of poets who have been.

3. *Create a* **map of the world,** *but instead of identifying countries, identify regions of the world by their most notable and prominent poets.*

   - Fashion a compendium of poetry to accompany this map so that there is a sample poem to coincide with every writer.
   - Do one map for classic poets and one map for Hip-Hop.
     (Yes, Hip-Hop is a worldwide phenomenon.)

4. *Design a* **PowerPoint**™ *presentation that identifies a timeline of classic poets who have been imprisoned, jailed, tortured or killed simply due to the words they have put on paper.*

   - Present both the poems and an explanation of why this particular piece cause so many problems.
   - See if there are any Hip-Hop poets who have suffered similar fates.

Gifted and Talented Education
G.A.TE. Differentiation *continued*

Unique Projects for Gifted and Talented Students

5. *Create a* **photo gallery** *that explores poetry through visual images.*

- Address theme, style, use of color, texture and overall subject matter.
- Determine if Hip-Hop poets can be illustrated through classic works of art (not just contemporary images).
- Determine if classic poets can be illustrated through Hip-Hop works of art (not just classic images).

6. *Find a representative piece of music that matches well with a Hip-Hop poem and* **choreograph and perform a dance** *while one group member recites the poem.*

- Use a classic poem and see if it can be matched to a Hip-Hop beat.
- Use a Hip-Hop poem and see if it can be matched to a classical piece.

7. *Assume a poet is no longer with us (and some of them aren't).* **Give a eulogy** *for the poet (both Hip-Hop and Classic) on the day of the unveiling of the tombstone.*

- This can accompany the presentation of an epitaph.

English Language Learners
Bridging Comprehension

I. *Have the English Language Learner bring in a poem written in his or her native tongue.*

- Resources to locate native language poems include:
  a. the student's family
  b. the internet
  c. the local or school library.

NOTE: An educator may want to secure a few poems on his or her own just in case a student does not locate appropriate material.

II. *Have the student translate the poem from their native tongue into English.*

- A Foreign Language Dictionary will be needed.
- Verse that rhymes in native languages may not rhyme when translated.

III. *Have the student identify poetic elements being used by the writer of the poem.*

- Refer to other parts of this book for tools and lessons.

IV. *Have the student interpret the basic meaning of the poem in English.*

- Some sample prompts for comprehension are:
  a. Who is the speaker?
  b. What is their tone?
  c. Did anything significant happen in the poem?
  d. Did you like the poem?

V. *Have students identify any cultural connections in the poem.*

- Is the poem representative of the student's home life in any way?
- Their parent's careers?
- The city or country from which the immigrated?

VI. *Have students illustrate the poem using colored pencils, markers, paint, etc.*

- Have students explain their reason for their color choices and images.
  a. For example: I choose to illustrate the kitten in yellow because it was happy in the poem.

VII. *Have the student read the poem to the class.*

- Have them read the native poem.
- Have them follow by reading their English translation.
- Have them point out any differences, lost allusions, or subtle points that may have been lost in their translation.

The ultimate goal is to seek places to affirm and validate the cultural heritage and background of the student.

Extended Writing Activities
Create a Diamante Poem

Learning Objective: To have students gain flexibility in their approach to the use of language.
Standards Addressed: 9/10 W&O 1.3, 1.4; LRA 3.7, 11/12 W&O 1.1, 1.2; W 2.2
Materials needed: This Worksheet
Methodology: See below.

Diamante: A seven line, diamond-shaped poem based on contrasting words.

Example of a Diamante poem:

Music
dynamic and lively
dancing, moving, grooving
The volume and the pace shift directions
mellowing, softening, easing
quiet and calm
Silence

THE PATTERN IS CLEAR:

- Line 1 and Line 7: beginning and ending nouns that contrast with one another.
- Line 2 and Line 6: are two adjectives describing the beginning and ending nouns.
- Line 3 and Line 5: three participles (i.e., *-ing* or *-ed* words) also describing the nouns
- Line 4: the four word turning point phrase turning point.
  (**NOTE:** Make this fourth line one of transition.)

Getting students started with Diamante poem is simple— have them think in terms of opposites.

For Example:

Happy/Sad – Wonderful/Terrible – Beautiful/Ugly

_____

_____   _____

_____   _____   _____

_____   _____   _____   _____

_____   _____   _____

_____   _____

_____

Poetry Writing Exercise:
Food as a Metaphor for Ourselves

Learning Objective: Students will identify and utilize the poetic device of metaphor.
Standards Addressed: 9/10 W&O 1.3, 1.4; LRA 3.7, 3.11; R 1.1, 1.2 11/12 LRA 3.4; W&O 1.1, 1.2; W 2.2
Materials Needed: Blank sheet of paper.
Methodology: See below.

ACTIVITY

Write a poem using food as a metaphor to describe yourself.

I. *Have each student develop a vocabulary around the foods they eat.*

Stress that they should think of foods that are unique to them, their family or their culture. (They can also write poems using their favorite foods.) Develop a large list of foods. Make sure they include breakfast, lunch, dinner and snack foods, but most especially, foods that REPRESENT them or their cultural background in some way or another. Be specific.

For example:

> pasta, marinara, eggplant parm, pesto, artichokes, olives, tomatoes, pizza, meatballs, cereal, ham, turkey, Doritos, root beer…

II. *Using words from the food vocabulary, write a poem describing yourself.*

III. *After each metaphor, ask them to write a supporting sentence (or sentence fragment) to further explain the metaphor they chose. (This step is for more advanced classes).*

For example:

> My hair is spaghetti. Its sticky curves rest on my shoulders.
> My heart is a tomato, juicy and ripe.

IV. *To help move this activity along a bit easier, the instructor can make a list of things that might be described in their poems on the board.*

Some things include:

> Face (looks), heart, brain, legs, eyes, hair, hands, fingers…

To kick this exercise up a notch—encourage them to include emotions, dreams, desires, feelings, fears, hopes and aspirations.

For example:

> My hair is spaghetti.
> Its sticky curves rest on my shoulders.
>
> My eyes are meatballs.
> My pupils are olives.
>
> My heart is a tomato,
> juicy and ripe.
>
> Desire is the sauce
> that pumps through my veins.
>
> My dream is a bubbling pizza,
> the toppings are my hopes.

Poetry Writing Exercise
Rewriting for Meaning

Learning Objective: Students will create a poem using poetic device of imagery.
Standards Addressed: 9/10 W&O 1.3, 1.4; LRA 3.7, 11/12 W&O 1.1, 1.2
Materials Needed: This worksheet.
Methodology: Create a "Me Against the World" poem.

ACTIVITY

Pick a favorite song and rewrite the lyrics with images and objects from the student's own life.

For example:

Rewrite Tupac Shakur's "Me Against the World."

I. Rewrite Tupac's "Me Against the World." Go line for line and rewrite the poem. Use things that are meaningful to you, and say the lines in a new way.

For example:

With all this extra stressin
COULD BE REWRITTEN as: ***With the blur of school, parents and a headache...***

II. On the blank lines below the original lines, write your new lines. When you are finished, you can rewrite your poem on a separate sheet of paper to make it your own!

"Me Against the World" by _____

With all this extra stressin _____
The question I wonder is after death, _____
after my last breath _____
When will I finally get to rest? _____
And those that possess, _____
steal from the ones without possessions _____
The message I stress: _____
to make it stop study your lessons _____
Don't settle for less — _____
even the genius asks questions _____
Be grateful for blessings. _____
Don't ever change, keep your essence _____
The power is in the people and politics we address _____
Always do your best, _____
don't let the pressure make you panic _____
And when you get stranded and _____
things don't go the way you planned it _____
Dreamin of riches, _____
in a position of makin a difference _____
Politicians and hypocrites, they don't wanna listen _____
If I'm insane, it's the fame made a brother change _____
It's just me against the world. _____

Poetry Writing Exercise
Rewriting with Opposite Imagery

Learning Objective: Students will identify and utilize the poetic device of imagery.
Standards Addressed: 9/10 W&O 1.3, 1.4; LRA 3.7, 3.11; 11/12 W&O 1.1, 1.2; W 1.5, 2.2
Materials Needed: This worksheet.
Methodology: See below.

ACTIVITY

Pick a favorite poem and rewrite the poetry with images and objects from the student's own life.

For example:
> Rewrite Langston Hughes' "Harlem: A Dream Deferred" using Opposite Imagery.

I. Rewrite Langston Hughes' "Dream Deferred," BUT USE OPPOSITE IMAGERY.

Go line for line and rewrite the poem.
Use the same senses the author uses, but use opposite images.
  For example:
  > *Does it dry up / like a raisin in the sun*
  > COULD BE CHANGED TO: Does it sweat wet / like an athlete in a sauna

II. On the blank lines below the original poem's lines, write your opposites.

When you are finished, you can rewrite your poem on a separate sheet of paper to make it your own!

"A Dream" by _____

What happens to a dream deferred? _____ ?

Does it dry up _____

like a raisin in the sun _____

Or fester like a sore— _____

And the run? _____ ?

Does it stink like rotten meat? _____ ?

Or crust and sugar over— _____

Like a syrupy sweet? _____ ?

Maybe it just sags _____

like a heavy load. _____ .

Or does it explode? _____ ?

Poetry Writing Exercise
The Alliterative Day in a Life

Learning Objective: Students will identify and utilize the poetic device of alliteration.
Standards Addressed: 9/10 W&O 1.3, 1.4; LRA 3.7, 11/12 W&O 1.1, 1.2
Materials needed: Blank sheet of paper.
Methodology: See below.

Alliteration: The repetition of the same or similar consonant sounds in words that are close together.

For example:

> "Behemoth, biggest born of earth, upheaved his vastness."
> *(John Milton)*

ACTIVITY

Alliterate a day in your life from rise and shine to nighty-night.

I. *Students will write a poem about a day in their lives, starting at the minute they wake up and working through until the minute they go to sleep at night.*

II. *They will use **ALLITERATION** as the main poetic device to tell their stories.*

III. PATTERN OPTION: *Shift the alliterative sound over the course of each section of the day.*

For example:

A sounds.	From the moment they wake up to when they get on the school bus.
B sounds.	From the moment they arrive at school to the bell for the first class
C sounds.	From the first classes to lunch
D sounds.	Lunch
E sounds.	Lunch to the end of school
F sounds.	When you get home after school
G sounds.	From homework to sleep

For example:

> When I wake with water in my eyes
> I pour whole, white milk on my Wheaties.
> Wonderful!
> What a way to start my day!
> Then I wash and walk to my wardrobe
> hanging like willow leaves in an old forgotten forest.
>
> I sit at the stop and see students rush to get a seat.
> It's icy slick and sleek on the streets
> One sad sap sleeps,
> Students sneak up to the snoozer and stick stuff in his snothole.